Higher
Maths

PAST PAPER SOLUTIONS
2012/13 Edition

Steven O'Hagan
George Kinnear

Higher Still Notes

ISBN: 978 0 9557067 5 2

Published by Higher Still Notes
www.hsn.uk.net

Note: The contents of this book have not been checked or approved by the Scottish Qualifications Authority. They reflect the authors' opinion of good answers to exam questions and have been checked against publicly available marking instructions.

Printed by Bell & Bain Ltd., Glasgow, Scotland, UK.

Contents

Introduction

How to use this book

Past papers are probably the best practice you can get for the actual exam, so you should plan to do as many as possible. Make sure you practice doing a whole paper in the allocated time, so you can get used to the pace.

The best way to use this book is for checking your answers *after* you have tried the questions yourself. Don't just read the solutions whenever you get stuck!

Here are some features of the book which should help you:

Questions and parts

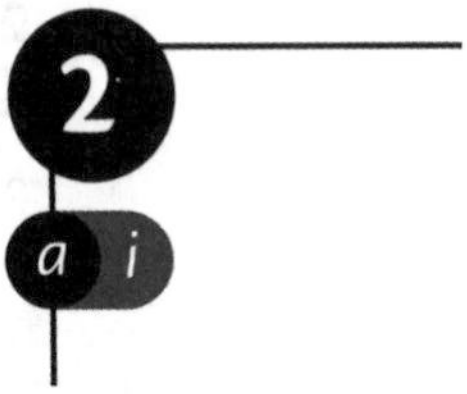

The question number is shown in the big circle, making it easy to spot at a glance.

All the parts of the question, including subparts, are also labelled.

References to notes

The grey box at the start of each solution has pointers to useful sections of our free Higher Maths notes (see below for details).

The "§" symbol just means "section", so the example to the right says you should look up Section 3 in the notes for Integration.

Clouds

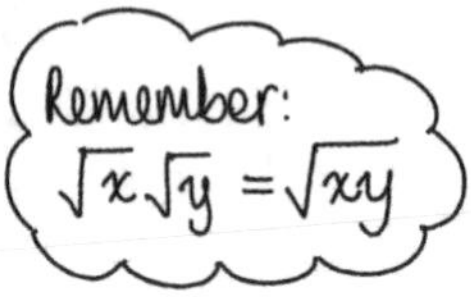

You'll notice these in a lot of solutions.

They usually contain helpful reminders, or explanations of the steps in the working.

Get more help with Higher Maths

You can download a free set of Higher Maths notes on our website:

www.hsn.uk.net/Higher-Maths

and you can also join our online forum, where you can chat with other students and ask about any questions you're stuck on:

www.hsn.uk.net/forum

Frequency Grid

	2008		2008 SQP		2009		2010		2011		2012	
	P1	P2	P1	P2	P1	P2	P1	P2	P1	P2	P1	P2
Straight Lines	7	1	1, 3, 11		3, 5, 15, 21		1, 21a,b	5a	2, 8, 21		4, 23	
Functions and Graphs	8, 17, 19, 20, 23a	3a	14		10, 14, 23	2a, 5a	4, 11, 20		3, 20	2a,b	9	1a, 4b, 5b
Differentiation	21a,c, 22	6	12, 21	3, 5, 7	4, 8, 20	1, 2b	12, 15, 17	5b	4, 22		2, 6, 8, 12, 18	3, 4a
Sequences	1, 4		2, 8		1, 6		2, 7			3	1	6
Polynomials and Quadratics	10, 13, 16, 21b		4, 5, 7, 17	2	12, 19	3a	5, 6, 13, 16, 18, 22		5, 7, 9, 17, 18	2c,d	3, 13, 19, 21a	1b, 5b
Integration		7	20, 25	9	16	5c	14	6c	11, 16	4	11, 21b	
Trigonometry	6, 9	5	9, 23, 24		7, 11, 24	5b	23	4	10, 12, 23	6b	5	6
Circles	2, 5	4		6	2, 9	4	8	3	6	7		2
Vectors	3, 11, 12, 18	2	10, 15, 16	1	17, 22	7	3, 10, 21c	1	1, 14, 15	1	7, 10, 15, 17	5a
Further Calculus	14, 15	3c	6, 18, 19		18		9	6a	13	6b	14, 16	
Exponentials and Logarithms	23b		13, 22	8	10	3b, 6	19	7	19	5	20	7
Wave Functions		3b		4	13			2		6a	22	

Formulae List

Circle

The equation $x^2+y^2+2gx+2fy+c=0$ represents a circle centre $(-g,-f)$ and radius $\sqrt{g^2+f^2-c}$.

The equation $(x-a)^2+(y-b)^2=r^2$ represents a circle centre (a,b) and radius r.

Scalar Product

$\boldsymbol{a}.\boldsymbol{b}=|\boldsymbol{a}||\boldsymbol{b}|\cos\theta$ where θ is the angle between $\boldsymbol{a}$ and $\boldsymbol{b}$.

or $\boldsymbol{a}.\boldsymbol{b}=a_1b_1+a_2b_2+a_3b_3$ where $\boldsymbol{a}=\begin{pmatrix}a_1\\a_2\\a_3\end{pmatrix}$ and $\boldsymbol{b}=\begin{pmatrix}b_1\\b_2\\b_3\end{pmatrix}$.

Trigonometric formulae

$$\sin(A\pm B)=\sin A\cos B\pm\cos A\sin B$$

$$\cos(A\pm B)=\cos A\cos B\mp\sin A\sin B$$

$$\sin 2A=2\sin A\cos A$$

$$\begin{aligned}\cos 2A&=\cos^2 A-\sin^2 A\\&=2\cos^2 A-1\\&=1-2\sin^2 A\end{aligned}$$

Table of standard derivatives

$f(x)$	$f'(x)$
$\sin ax$	$a\cos ax$
$\cos ax$	$-a\sin ax$

Table of standard integrals

$f(x)$	$\int f(x)\,dx$
$\sin ax$	$-\frac{1}{a}\cos ax+c$
$\cos ax$	$\frac{1}{a}\sin ax+c$

2008 Paper 1

1

See **Sequences** §2

$u_{11} = 0\cdot3u_{10} + 6 = 0\cdot3 \times 10 + 6 = 3 + 6 = 9.$

$u_{12} = 0\cdot3u_{11} + 6 = 0\cdot3 \times 9 + 6 = 2\cdot7 + 6 = 8\cdot7.$

C

2

See **Circles** §1

Since the x-axis is a tangent, the radius is 6 units.

Therefore the equation is

$$(x-(-7))^2 + (y-6)^2 = 6^2$$

$$(x+7)^2 + (y-6)^2 = 36.$$

The circle with centre (a, b) and radius r has equation: $(x-a)^2 + (y-b)^2 = r^2$.

D

3

See **Vectors** §13

$$\underline{u}.\underline{v} = (k \times 0) + (-1 \times 4) + (1 \times k)$$

$$= k - 4.$$

Since $\underline{u}$ and $\underline{v}$ are perpendicular, $\underline{u}.\underline{v} = 0$.

So $k - 4 = 0$ i.e. $k = 4$.

C

4

See **Sequences** §4

<u>Method 1</u> $\quad l = \dfrac{b}{1-a}$ with $a = 0\cdot4$ and $b = -240$.

$$l = \frac{-240}{1-0\cdot4} = -\frac{240}{0\cdot6} = -\frac{2400}{6} = -400.$$

<u>Method 2</u> As $n \to \infty$, $u_{n+1} = u_n = l$.

So $l = 0\cdot4l - 240$

$0\cdot6l = -240$

$$l = -\frac{240}{0\cdot6} = -\frac{2400}{6} = -400.$$

B

5

See **Circles** §6

$m_{radius} = \frac{9-5}{7-2} = \frac{4}{5}$.

So $m_{tangent} = -\frac{5}{4}$ since the radius and tangent are perpendicular.

The equation of the tangent is:

$y - 9 = -\frac{5}{4}(x-7)$ using point (7,9)

A

6

See **Trigonometry** §1

$2\sin x - \sqrt{3} = 0$

$\sin x = \frac{\sqrt{3}}{2}$

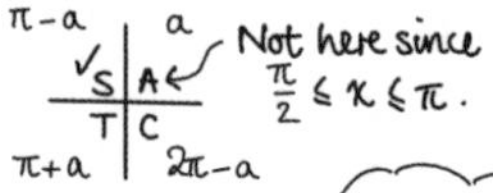

$x = \pi - \frac{\pi}{3}$

$= \frac{2\pi}{3}$

$a = \sin^{-1}\left(\frac{\sqrt{3}}{2}\right)$

$= \frac{\pi}{3}$.

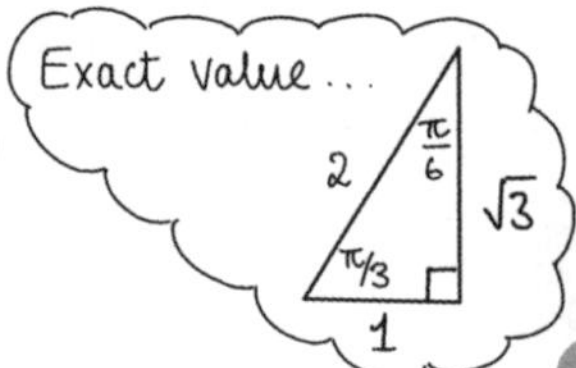

B

7

See **Straight Lines** §3

$m = \tan 135°$

$= -\tan 45°$

$= -1$.

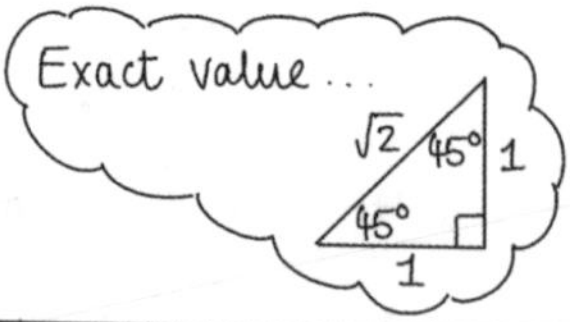

C

8

See **Functions and Graphs** §10

$y = -f(x-2)$ is $y = f(x)$ reflected in the x-axis and then shifted 2 places to the right.

D

9

See **Trigonometry** §3

$\sin a = \dfrac{\text{opp.}}{\text{hyp.}} = \dfrac{3}{5}$. So we have:

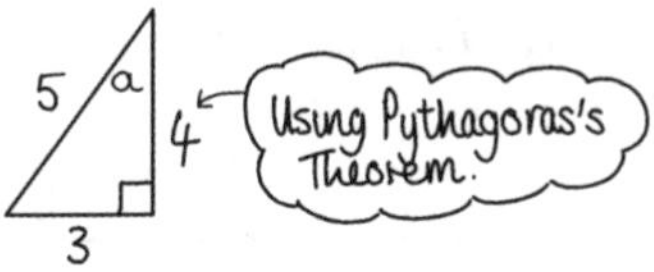

So $\cos a = \dfrac{\text{adj}}{\text{hyp.}} = \dfrac{4}{5}$.

Now $\sin(x+a) = \sin x\cos a + \cos x\sin a$

$= \frac{4}{5}\sin x + \frac{3}{5}\cos x$.

B

10

See **Polynomials and Quadratics** §2

The discriminant is $b^2 - 4ac = 1 - 4\times1\times1 = -3$.

Since $b^2 - 4ac < 0$, the roots are <u>not</u> real and <u>not</u> equal.

A

11

See **Vectors** §10

$$\overrightarrow{EP} = \underline{p} - \underline{e} = \begin{pmatrix}1\\5\\7\end{pmatrix} - \begin{pmatrix}-2\\-1\\4\end{pmatrix} = \begin{pmatrix}3\\6\\3\end{pmatrix}$$

$$\overrightarrow{PF} = \underline{f} - \underline{p} = \begin{pmatrix}7\\17\\13\end{pmatrix} - \begin{pmatrix}1\\5\\7\end{pmatrix} = \begin{pmatrix}6\\12\\6\end{pmatrix} = 2\overrightarrow{EP}$$

So $\dfrac{EP}{PF} = \dfrac{1}{2}$, i.e. P divides EF in the ratio 1 : 2.

B

12

See **Vectors** §5

From the diagram, $\overrightarrow{VT} = \overrightarrow{VW} + \overrightarrow{WS} + \overrightarrow{ST}$

$$= -\underline{f} - \underline{h} + \underline{g}$$

$$= -\underline{f} + \underline{g} - \underline{h}.$$

C

13

See **Polynomials and Quadratics** §5

Since the parabola crosses the x-axis at 1 and 4, the equation has the form

$$y = k(x-1)(x-4).$$

Since (0,12) lies on the parabola,

$$12 = k \times (-1) \times (-4)$$

$$k = \frac{12}{4}$$

$$= 3.$$

So the equation is $y = 3(x-1)(x-4)$.

A

14

See **Further Calculus** §6

$$\int 4\sin(2x+3)\,dx = -4 \times \tfrac{1}{2}\cos(2x+3) + c$$

$$= -2\cos(2x+3) + c.$$

Using:
$\int \sin(ax+b)\,dx$
$= -\frac{1}{a}\cos(ax+b) + c$

B

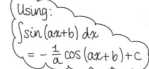

2008

15

See **Further Calculus** §4

Using the chain rule,

$$\frac{d}{dx}(x^3+4)^2 = 2(x^3+4) \times \frac{d}{dx}(x^3+4)$$
$$= 2(x^3+4) \times (3x^2)$$
$$= 6x^2(x^3+4).$$

C

16

See **Polynomials and Quadratics** §3

Method 1 Compensating...

$$2x^2+4x+7 = 2(x^2+2x)+7$$
$$= 2(x+1)^2 - 2 + 7 = 2(x+1)^2+5. \quad \text{So } q = 5.$$

This gives the correct x^2 and x terms, and an extra 2.

Take off this extra 2.

Method 2 Comparing coefficients...

$$2x^2+4x+7 = 2(x+p)^2+q$$
$$= 2x^2+4px+2p^2+q$$

So $4p = 4$, $p = 1$ and $2p^2+q = 7$, $q = 7-2p^2 = 5$

A

17

See **Functions and Graphs** §2

We need $9-x^2 \geq 0$

$x^2 \leq 9$

$-3 \leq x \leq 3.$

Remember: we can't take the square root of a negative number.

C

2008

18

See **Vectors** §14

$$\underset{\sim}{q}\cdot(\underset{\sim}{p}+\underset{\sim}{q}) = \underset{\sim}{q}\cdot\underset{\sim}{p} + \underset{\sim}{q}\cdot\underset{\sim}{q}$$
$$= \underset{\sim}{p}\cdot\underset{\sim}{q} + |\underset{\sim}{q}|^2$$
$$= 10 + 4^2$$
$$= 26.$$

Remember:
- $\underset{\sim}{a}\cdot\underset{\sim}{b} = \underset{\sim}{b}\cdot\underset{\sim}{a}$
- $\underset{\sim}{a}\cdot\underset{\sim}{a} = |\underset{\sim}{a}|^2$

C

19

See **Functions and Graphs** §5

Since $(3,54)$ lies on the curve, $54 = 2m^3$

$$m^3 = 27$$
$$m = \sqrt[3]{27}$$
$$= 3$$

B

20

See **Functions and Graphs** §6

Since $(q, 2)$ lies on the curve, $2 = \log_3(q-4)$

$$q-4 = 3^2$$
$$q = 9+4$$
$$= 13.$$

Remember:
$y = \log_a x$
$\Leftrightarrow x = a^y$

D

21

(a) See **Differentiation** §7 and §8
(b) See **Polynomials and Quadratics** §9
(c) See **Differentiation** §9

a Stationary points exist where $f'(x)=0$

$$f'(x) = 3x^2 - 3 = 0$$
$$3x^2 = 3$$
$$x = \pm 1.$$

When $x = -1$, $y = (-1)^3 - 3\times(-1) + 2$
$= -1 + 3 + 2$
$= 4$ $\quad(-1,4)$

When $x = 1$, $y = 1 - 3 + 2 = 0$ $\quad(1,0)$.

cont...

Method 1 Nature table:

x	-1^-	-1	-1^+	1^-	1	1^+
$f'(x)$	+	0	–	–	0	+
Sketch	/	—	\	\	_	/

Method 2 Second derivative test: $f''(x) = 6x$

$f''(-1) = -6 < 0$ and $f''(1) = 6 > 0$.

So $(-1,4)$ is a maximum turning point
$(1,0)$ is a minimum turning point.

b i **Method 1** From part (a), $f(1) = 0$ (ie $x = 1$ is a root) and so $(x-1)$ is a factor.

Method 2 Using synthetic division...

1	1	0	−3	2
		1	1	−2
	1	1	−2	0

Since the remainder is 0, $x = 1$ is a root so $(x-1)$ is a factor.

ii $x^3 - 3x + 2 = (x-1)(x^2 + x - 2)$ ← Either by inspection or from the bottom row of the table.
$= (x-1)(x-1)(x+2)$

c x-axis (i.e. $y = 0$). From above, $x = -2, 1$.
Hence the curve crosses the x-axis at $(-2,0)$ and $(1,0)$.

y-axis (i.e. $x = 0$). $f(0) = 2$
Hence the curve crosses the y-axis at $(0,2)$.

Using this information, and the stationary points,

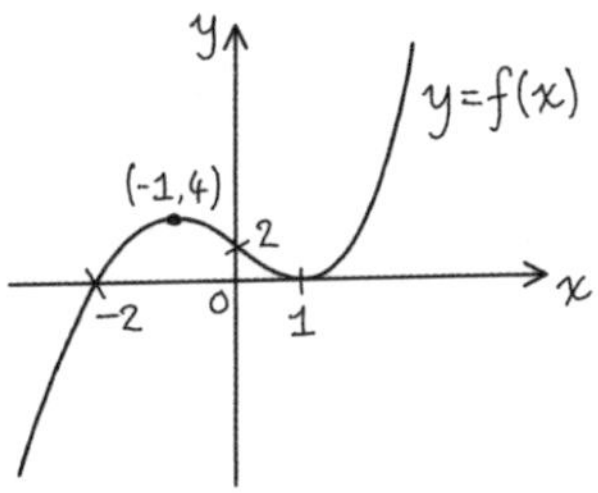

22

(a) See **Differentiation** §5, (b) See **Straight Lines** §6

a $\frac{dy}{dx} = 3x^2 - 12x + 8$

Remember: $\frac{dy}{dx} = m_{\text{tangent}}$

So
$$3x^2 - 12x + 8 = -1$$
$$3x^2 - 12x + 9 = 0$$
$$x^2 - 4x + 3 = 0$$
$$(x-1)(x-3) = 0$$
$$x = 1 \text{ or } x = 3$$

When $x = 1$, $y = 1 - 6 + 8 = 3$

When $x = 3$, $y = 3^3 - 6 \times 3^2 + 8 \times 3 = 27 - 54 + 24 = -3$.

So the points are $(1,3)$ and $(3,-3)$.

b The line $y = 4 - x$ has gradient -1.
So A must be one of the points found in part (a).

Remember: the line $y = mx + c$ has gradient m.

The equation is only satisfied by $(1,3)$, since $3 = 4 - 1$, and so A is the point $(1,3)$.

23

(a) See **Functions and Graphs** §3
(b) See **Exponentials and Logarithms** §5

a $h(f(x)) = h(x^2 - x + 10) = \log_2(x^2 - x + 10)$.

$h(g(x)) = h(5 - x) = \log_2(5 - x)$.

b
$$\log_2(x^2 - x + 10) - \log_2(5 - x) = 3$$
$$\log_2\left(\frac{x^2 - x + 10}{5 - x}\right) = 3$$
$$\frac{x^2 - x + 10}{5 - x} = 2^3$$
$$x^2 - x + 10 = 40 - 8x$$
$$x^2 + 7x - 30 = 0$$
$$(x + 10)(x - 3) = 0$$
$$x = -10 \text{ or } x = 3.$$

Remember:
- $\log_a x - \log_a y = \log_a \frac{x}{y}$
- $\log_a x = y \Leftrightarrow x = a^y$

2008 Paper 2

1

See **Straight Lines** – (a) §9, (b) §7, (c) §10

a $\text{midpoint}_{BC} = \left(\frac{-3+5}{2}, \frac{-1-5}{2}\right) = (1,-3).$

$m_{BC} = \frac{-5-(-1)}{5-(-3)} = \frac{-4}{8} = -\frac{1}{2}$. So $m_{\perp} = 2$ since $m_{BC} \times m_{\perp} = -1$.

So the equation is

$$y+3 = 2(x-1) \quad \text{using point } (1,-3)$$
$$y+3 = 2x-2$$
$$y = 2x-5$$

b $\text{midpoint}_{AB} = \left(\frac{7-3}{2}, \frac{9-1}{2}\right) = (2,4).$

$m_{med} = \frac{-5-4}{5-2} = \frac{-9}{3} = -3.$

So the equation is

$$y+5 = -3(x-5) \quad \text{using } C(5,-5).$$
$$y+5 = -3x+15$$
$$y = -3x+10.$$

c Solve simultaneously...

Method 1 Eliminating y:

$$y = 2x-5 \quad \text{——— ①}$$
$$y = -3x+10 \quad \text{——— ②}$$

①−②: $5x - 15 = 0$

$$x = 3.$$

Method 2 Equating:

$$2x-5 = -3x+10$$
$$5x = 15$$
$$x = 3.$$

When $x=3$, $y = 2\times3-5 = 1$. So the point of intersection is $(3,1)$

2

See **Vectors** – *(a) §7 and §10, (b) §7, (c) §12*

a From the diagram, $A(8,0,0)$, $C(0,4,0)$, $E(8,0,6)$ and $G(0,4,6)$.

So $\underline{p} = \underline{a} + \frac{2}{3}\overrightarrow{AE} = \begin{pmatrix} 8 \\ 0 \\ 0 \end{pmatrix} + \frac{2}{3}\begin{pmatrix} 0 \\ 0 \\ 6 \end{pmatrix} = \begin{pmatrix} 8 \\ 0 \\ 4 \end{pmatrix}$

$\underline{q} = \underline{c} + \frac{1}{2}\overrightarrow{CG} = \begin{pmatrix} 0 \\ 4 \\ 0 \end{pmatrix} + \frac{1}{2}\begin{pmatrix} 0 \\ 0 \\ 6 \end{pmatrix} = \begin{pmatrix} 0 \\ 4 \\ 3 \end{pmatrix}$.

Note: you don't need to show this working.

Hence $P(8,0,4)$ and $Q(0,4,3)$.

b $\overrightarrow{PQ} = \underline{q} - \underline{p} = \begin{pmatrix} 0 \\ 4 \\ 3 \end{pmatrix} - \begin{pmatrix} 8 \\ 0 \\ 4 \end{pmatrix} = \begin{pmatrix} -8 \\ 4 \\ -1 \end{pmatrix}$

$\overrightarrow{PA} = \underline{a} - \underline{p} = \begin{pmatrix} 8 \\ 0 \\ 0 \end{pmatrix} - \begin{pmatrix} 8 \\ 0 \\ 4 \end{pmatrix} = \begin{pmatrix} 0 \\ 0 \\ -4 \end{pmatrix}$

Remember: $\overrightarrow{AB} = \underline{b} - \underline{a}$.

c $|\overrightarrow{PQ}| = \sqrt{(-8)^2 + 4^2 + (-1)^2} = \sqrt{81} = 9$.

$|\overrightarrow{PA}| = \sqrt{(-4)^2} = 4$

Method 1 $\cos Q\hat{P}A = \dfrac{\overrightarrow{PQ}.\overrightarrow{PA}}{|\overrightarrow{PQ}||\overrightarrow{PA}|}$

Using: $\underline{a}.\underline{b} = |\underline{a}||\underline{b}|\cos\theta$

$= \dfrac{-8\times0 + 4\times0 - 1\times(-4)}{9\times4}$

$= \dfrac{1}{9}$

$Q\hat{P}A = \cos^{-1}\left(\frac{1}{9}\right)$

$= 83{\cdot}62^\circ$ (to 2 d.p.)

OR $1{\cdot}459$ rads (to 3 d.p.)

Method 2 $|\overrightarrow{AQ}| = \left|\begin{pmatrix} -8 \\ 4 \\ 3 \end{pmatrix}\right| = \sqrt{89}$.

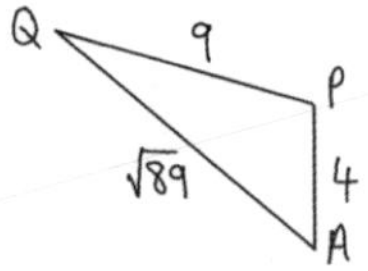

$\cos Q\hat{P}A = \dfrac{81 + 16 - 89}{2\times9\times4}$

$= \dfrac{1}{9}$

Remember the cosine rule: $\cos A = \dfrac{b^2 + c^2 - a^2}{2bc}$

So $Q\hat{P}A = 83{\cdot}62^\circ$ (to 2 d.p.) OR $1{\cdot}459$ rads (to 3 d.p.)

3

(a) See **Functions and Graphs** *§9 and §10*
(b) See **Wave Functions** *§2*
(c) See **Further Calculus** *§1*

a i The amplitude is $\sqrt{7}$ so $p = \sqrt{7}$.

ii The amplitude is 3 but the sine graph has also been reflected in the x-axis.

Hence $q = -3$.

b
$$\begin{aligned} f(x) + g(x) &= \sqrt{7}\cos x - 3\sin x \\ &= k\cos(x + a) \\ &= k\cos x\cos a - k\sin x\sin a \\ &= (k\cos a)\cos x - (k\sin a)\sin x \end{aligned}$$

Comparing coefficients: $k\sin a = 3$, $k\cos a = \sqrt{7}$

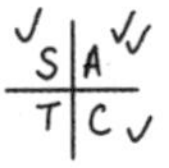

So $k = \sqrt{3^2 + \sqrt{7}^2} = \sqrt{16} = 4$ and $\tan a = \dfrac{k\sin a}{k\cos a} = \dfrac{3}{\sqrt{7}}$

$a = \tan^{-1}\left(\dfrac{3}{\sqrt{7}}\right) = 0{\cdot}848$ (to 3 d.p.)

So $f(x) + g(x) = 4\cos(x + 0{\cdot}848)$.

c
$$\begin{aligned} f'(x) + g'(x) &= \frac{d}{dx}\big(f(x) + g(x)\big) \\ &= \frac{d}{dx}\big(4\cos(x + 0{\cdot}848)\big) \\ &= -4\sin(x + 0{\cdot}848). \end{aligned}$$

Using: $\dfrac{d}{dx}\cos x = -\sin x$.

4

See **Circles** *– (a) §3, (b) §1 and §7, (c) §4*

a Comparing with $x^2 + y^2 + 2gx + 2fy + c = 0$,

$2g = 8$, $2f = 4$ and $c = -38$
$g = 4$ $f = 2$.

The centre is $(-4, -2)$.

The radius is $\sqrt{16 + 4 + 38} = \sqrt{58}$ units.

The circle $x^2 + y^2 + 2gx + 2fy + c = 0$ has centre $(-g, -f)$ and radius $\sqrt{g^2 + f^2 - c}$.

cont...

b The circle $(x-4)^2+(y-6)^2=26$ has centre $(4,6)$ and radius $\sqrt{26}$ units.

The distance between the centres is

$$d=\sqrt{(4+4)^2+(6+2)^2}=\sqrt{128}=8\sqrt{2} \text{ units.}$$

The sum of the two radii is larger than d since:

$$\sqrt{58}+\sqrt{26}=\underbrace{\sqrt{13}}_{>3}\sqrt{2}+\underbrace{\sqrt{29}}_{>5}\sqrt{2}>8\sqrt{2}=d.$$

Since the distance between the centres is less than the sum of the radii, the circles intersect.

c Put $y=4-x$ in the equation of one of the circles:

$$x^2+(4-x)^2+8x+4(4-x)-38=0$$
$$x^2+16-8x+x^2+8x+16-4x-38=0$$
$$2x^2-4x-6=0$$
$$x^2-2x-3=0$$
$$(x+1)(x-3)=0$$
$$x=-1 \text{ or } x=3.$$

When $x=-1$, $y=4-(-1)=5$.
When $x=3$, $y=4-3=1$.

So the points of intersection are $(-1,5)$ and $(3,1)$.

5

See **Trigonometry** §4 and §5

$$\cos 2x° + 2\sin x° = \sin^2 x°$$
$$1-2\sin^2 x° + 2\sin x° = \sin^2 x°$$
$$3\sin^2 x° - 2\sin x° - 1 = 0$$
$$(3\sin x°+1)(\sin x°-1)=0$$

Using: $\cos 2A = 1-2\sin^2 A$

$3\sin x°+1=0$

$\sin x° = -\frac{1}{3}$

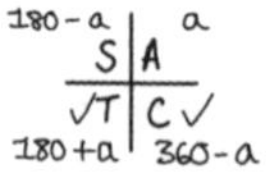

or $\sin x°-1=0$

$\sin x°=1$

$x=90$

$$a=\sin^{-1}\left(\frac{1}{3}\right)$$
$$=19.47 \text{ (to 2 d.p.)}$$

$x=180+19.47$ or $360-19.47$ or 90

$=199.47$ or 340.53 or 90

6

(a) See **Straight Lines** *§6*
(b) See **Polynomials and Quadratics** *§4 or* **Differentiation** *§12*

a The line has gradient −2 and y-axis intercept 6.
So its equation is $y = -2x + 6$.

The length QR is the y-coordinate of the point on this line with x-coordinate t, i.e.

$$QR = -2t + 6 = 6 - 2t.$$

b The area of the rectangle is given by $A = \text{length} \times \text{breadth}$
$= t(6-2t)$.

Method 1 Sketch $A = t(6-2t)$.

Crosses t-axis when $t(6-2t) = 0$

$t = 0$ or $6 - 2t = 0$

$t = 3$

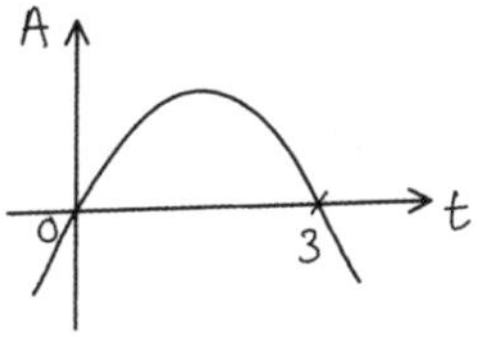

The parabola is concave down (∩-shaped) because the coefficient of t^2 is negative.

The maximum lies mid-way between the roots, ie when $t = \frac{3}{2}$.

Method 2 $A = 6t - 2t^2$.

Stationary points exist where $\frac{dA}{dt} = 0$.

$$\frac{dA}{dt} = 6 - 4t = 0$$
$$4t = 6$$
$$t = \frac{3}{2}$$

Nature:

t	$\frac{3}{2}^-$	$\frac{3}{2}$	$\frac{3}{2}^+$
$\frac{dA}{dt}$	+	0	−
Sketch	/	—	\

OR $\frac{d^2A}{dt^2} = -4$

Hence $t = \frac{3}{2}$ gives the maximum area.

When $t = \frac{3}{2}$, $QR = 6 - 2 \times \frac{3}{2} = 3$.

Hence Q is $\left(\frac{3}{2}, 3\right)$.

2008

7

See **Integration** §7 or §6

First notice that the shaded area is symmetrical about the y-axis. So first calculate the area for $x>0$, then double.

Method 1 Rearrange for x and integrate with respect to y.

$$y = 32 - 2x^2$$
$$2x^2 = 32 - y$$
$$x = \left(16 - \frac{y}{2}\right)^{1/2}$$

Only consider $x>0$.

So half the shaded area is given by

$$\int_{14}^{24} \left(16 - \tfrac{1}{2}y\right)^{1/2} dy = \left[\frac{\left(16 - \frac{y}{2}\right)^{3/2}}{\frac{3}{2} \times \left(-\frac{1}{2}\right)}\right]_{14}^{24}$$

$$= \left[-\frac{4}{3}\sqrt{16 - \frac{y}{2}}^{\,3}\right]_{14}^{24}$$

$$= -\frac{4}{3}\sqrt{4}^{\,3} + \frac{4}{3}\sqrt{9}^{\,3}$$

$$= \frac{76}{3} \quad \left(= 25\tfrac{1}{3}\right)$$

Remember: $\int (ax+b)^n \, dx = \frac{(ax+b)^{n+1}}{a(n+1)} + c$

Hence the shaded area is $\frac{152}{3}$ $\left(\text{or } 50\tfrac{2}{3}\right)$ square units.

cont...

Method 2

Find a and b.

a: $32 - 2x^2 = 24$
$2x^2 = 8$
$x = 2$

(Only consider $x > 0$.)

i.e. $a = 2$.

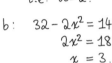

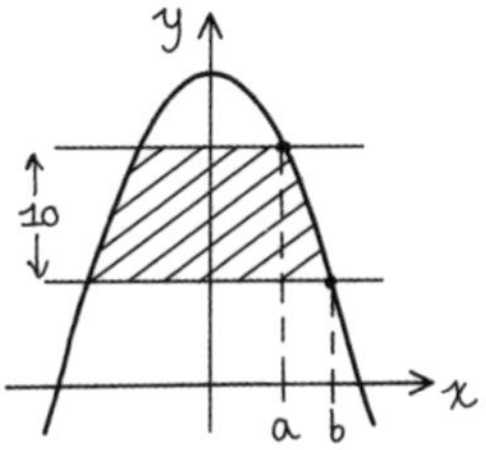

b: $32 - 2x^2 = 14$
$2x^2 = 18$
$x = 3$.

i.e. $b = 3$.

The shaded area between a and b is given by

$$\int_2^3 (\text{upper} - \text{lower})\,dx$$

$$= \int_2^3 (32 - 2x^2 - 14)\,dx$$

$$= \left[18x - \frac{2}{3}x^3\right]_2^3$$

$$= 54 - \frac{2}{3}\times 27 - 36 + \frac{2}{3}\times 8$$

$$= \frac{16}{3} \quad \left(= 5\frac{1}{3}\right)$$

So the total shaded area is

$$2\left(10\times 2 + \frac{16}{3}\right) = \frac{152}{3} \text{ or } 50\frac{2}{3} \text{ square units.}$$

2008 SQP Paper 1

1

See **Straight Lines** §3

$m_{PQ} = \frac{p-(-5)}{7-4} = \frac{p+5}{3}$.

So $\frac{p+5}{3} = 3$

$p+5 = 9$

$p = 4$.

B

2

See **Sequences** §2

$u_1 = u_0 + 5 = -3+5 = 2$

$u_2 = u_1 + 5 = 2+5 = 7$

C

3

See **Straight Lines** §6 and §5

$3y = -2x + 1$

$y = -\frac{2}{3}x + \frac{1}{3}$.

So the gradient is $m = -\frac{2}{3}$.

Remember: To extract the gradient, rearrange to the form $y = mx + c$.

Any line perpendicular has gradient $m_{\perp} = \frac{3}{2}$, since $m \times m_{\perp} = -1$.

C

4

See **Polynomials and Quadratics** §9

The remainder is

$f(-3) = (-3)^3 - (-3)^2 - 5 \times (-3) - 3$

$= -27 - 9 + 15 - 3$

$= -24$.

You could have used synthetic division

A

5

See **Polynomials and Quadratics** §3

Method 1 Compensating...

$$x^2-16x+27 = (x-8)^2-64+27 = (x-8)^2-37. \text{ So } q=-37.$$

This gives the correct x^2 and x terms, and an extra 64

Take off this extra 64

Method 2 Comparing coefficients...

$$x^2-16x+27 = (x+p)^2+q$$
$$= x^2+2px+p^2+q.$$

So $2p=-16$ and $p^2+q = 27$

$p=-8$ $\quad q = 27-p^2$

$= -37.$

A

6

See **Further Calculus** §4

Using the chain rule,

$$\frac{d}{dx}(8-2x^2)^{2/3} = \frac{2}{3}(8-2x^2)^{-1/3} \times \frac{d}{dx}(8-2x^2)$$
$$= \frac{2}{3}(8-2x^2)^{-1/3}.(-4x)$$
$$= -\frac{8}{3}(8-2x^2)^{-1/3}.$$

A

7

See **Polynomials and Quadratics** §9

Since the remainder is zero, $(x-1)$ is a factor, i.e.

$$f(x) = (x-1)(x^2-4x-5)$$
$$= (x-1)(x+1)(x-5).$$

D

8

See **Sequences** §4

<u>Method 1</u> $l = \frac{b}{1-a}$ with $a = 0{\cdot}4$ and $b = 3$

$$l = \frac{3}{1-0{\cdot}4} = \frac{3}{0{\cdot}6} = \frac{30}{6} = 5.$$

<u>Method 2</u> As $n \to \infty$, $u_{n+1} = u_n = l$.

So $l = 0{\cdot}4l + 3$

$0{\cdot}6l = 3$

$$l = \frac{3}{0{\cdot}6} = \frac{30}{6} = 5.$$

C

9

See **Trigonometry** §1

$\tan x = -\sqrt{3}$

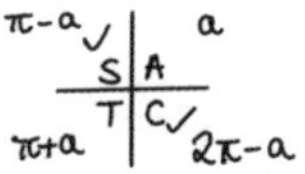

$$a = \tan^{-1}(\sqrt{3}) = \frac{\pi}{3}$$

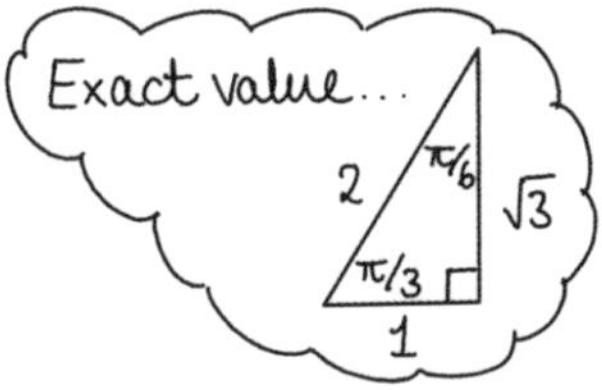

So $x = \pi - \frac{\pi}{3}$ or $2\pi - \frac{\pi}{3}$.

$= \frac{2\pi}{3}$ or $\frac{5\pi}{3}$.

C

10

See **Vectors** §10

$$\overrightarrow{PQ} = \underline{q} - \underline{p} = \begin{pmatrix} -1 \\ 8 \\ 3 \end{pmatrix} - \begin{pmatrix} -3 \\ 4 \\ 7 \end{pmatrix} = \begin{pmatrix} 2 \\ 4 \\ -4 \end{pmatrix}$$

$$\overrightarrow{QR} = \underline{r} - \underline{q} = \begin{pmatrix} 0 \\ 10 \\ 1 \end{pmatrix} - \begin{pmatrix} -1 \\ 8 \\ 3 \end{pmatrix} = \begin{pmatrix} 1 \\ 2 \\ -2 \end{pmatrix}$$

So $\overrightarrow{PQ} = 2\overrightarrow{QR}$, i.e. $\frac{PQ}{QR} = \frac{2}{1}$. Hence Q divides PR in the ratio 2:1.

A

11

See **Straight Lines** §6 and §3

$2y = x$

$y = \frac{1}{2}x$. So $m = \frac{1}{2}$.

Since $m = \tan p°$,

$\tan p° = \frac{1}{2}$

$p = \tan^{-1}\left(\frac{1}{2}\right)$

Remember:
To extract the gradient, rearrange to the form $y = mx + c$.

A

12

See **Differentiation** §6

$g'(x) = x^2 + 2x + 1$

$= (x+1)^2$

$\geqslant 0$.

Since $g'(x) \geqslant 0$ for all x, g is never decreasing.

D

13

See **Exponentials and Logarithms** §3

$\log_2(x+1) - 2\log_2 3 = \log_2(x+1) - \log_2 3^2$

$= \log_2(x+1) - \log_2 9$

$= \log_2\left(\frac{x+1}{9}\right)$

Remember:
- $k\log_a x = \log_a x^k$.
- $\log_a x - \log_a y = \log_a \frac{x}{y}$.

A

14

See **Functions and Graphs** §10

$y = -g(x)$ is $y = g(x)$ reflected in the x-axis.

$3 - g(x) = -g(x) + 3$.
So $y = 3 - g(x)$ is $y = -g(x)$ shifted up by 3.

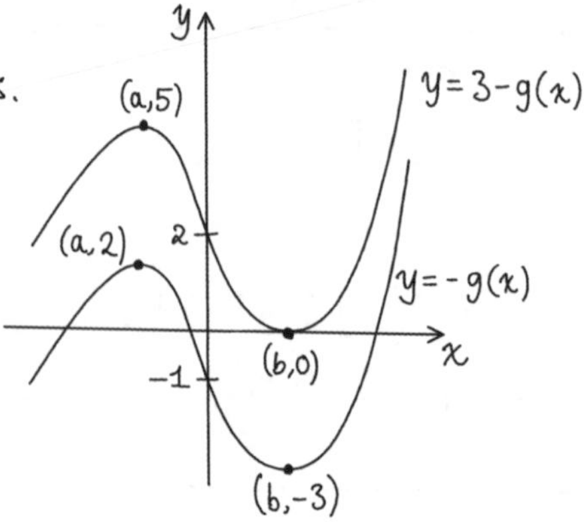

D

15

See **Vectors** §7 and §10

Method 1

$$\underline{t} = \underline{p} + \tfrac{1}{2}\overrightarrow{PQ}$$
$$= \underline{p} + \tfrac{1}{2}(\underline{q} - \underline{p})$$
$$= \tfrac{1}{2}(\underline{p} + \underline{q})$$
$$= \tfrac{1}{2}\left(\begin{pmatrix}1\\3\\-1\end{pmatrix} + \begin{pmatrix}2\\5\\1\end{pmatrix}\right)$$
$$= \begin{pmatrix}3/2\\4\\0\end{pmatrix}.$$

Method 2 Using the midpoint formula, T is

$$\left(\frac{1+2}{2}, \frac{3+5}{2}, \frac{-1+1}{2}\right) = \left(\frac{3}{2}, 4, 0\right).$$

So $\underline{t} = \begin{pmatrix}3/2\\4\\0\end{pmatrix}$.

B

16

See **Vectors** §7

$$\overrightarrow{AD} = 4\overrightarrow{AB}$$
$$\underline{d} - \underline{a} = 4(\underline{b} - \underline{a})$$
$$\underline{d} = 4\underline{b} - 4\underline{a} + \underline{a}$$
$$= 4\underline{b} - 3\underline{a}$$
$$= 4\begin{pmatrix}-1\\8\\3\end{pmatrix} - 3\begin{pmatrix}-3\\4\\7\end{pmatrix}$$
$$= \begin{pmatrix}-4\\32\\12\end{pmatrix} - \begin{pmatrix}-9\\12\\21\end{pmatrix}$$
$$= \begin{pmatrix}5\\20\\-9\end{pmatrix}.$$

So D has coordinates $(5, 20, -9)$.

D

17

See **Polynomials and Quadratics** §5

Since $(3,-18)$ lies on the parabola,

$$-18 = k \times 3 \times (3-6)$$
$$-18 = -9k$$
$$k = 2.$$

C

18

See **Further Calculus** §4

$$\frac{dy}{dx} = 3 \times (-5)\sin 5x$$
$$= -15\sin 5x.$$

Using: $\frac{d}{dx}(\cos ax) = -a\sin ax.$

B

19

See **Further Calculus** §5

$$\int (4x+1)^{1/2}\,dx = \frac{(4x+1)^{3/2}}{4 \times \frac{3}{2}} + c$$
$$= \frac{1}{6}(4x+1)^{3/2} + c.$$

Remember:
$\int (ax+b)^n\,dx = \frac{(ax+b)^{n+1}}{a(n+1)} + c$

A

20

See **Integration** §4

$$\int_0^1 (3x+1)^{-1/2}\,dx = \left[\frac{2}{3}\sqrt{3x+1}\right]_0^1$$
$$= \frac{2}{3} \times 2 - \frac{2}{3} \times 1$$
$$= \frac{2}{3}.$$

A

21

See **Differentiation** – (a) §7 and §8, (b) §9

a Stationary points exist where $\frac{dy}{dx} = 0$.

$$\frac{dy}{dx} = 3x^2 + 6x - 9 = 0$$
$$x^2 + 2x - 3 = 0$$
$$(x+3)(x-1) = 0$$
$$x = -3 \quad \text{or} \quad x = 1$$

When $x = -3$, $y = (-3)^3 + 3\times(-3)^2 - 9\times(-3) + 5$
$= -27 + 27 + 27 + 5$
$= 32$. $(-3, 32)$

When $x = 1$, $y = 1 + 3 - 9 + 5 = 0$ $(1, 0)$

Method 1 Nature table:

x	-3^-	-3	-3^+	1^-	1	1^+
$(x+3)$	−	0	+	+		+
$(x-1)$	−		−	−	0	+
$\frac{dy}{dx}$	+	0	−	−	0	+
Sketch	/	—	\	\	_	/

Method 2 Second derivative test: $\frac{d^2y}{dx^2} = 6x + 6$.

$f''(-3) = -12 < 0$ and $f''(1) = 12 > 0$

So $(-3, 32)$ is a maximum turning point
$(1, 0)$ is a minimum turning point.

b When $x = 0$, $y = 5$. So $(0, 5)$ lies on the curve.
Using the given information, and the stationary points,

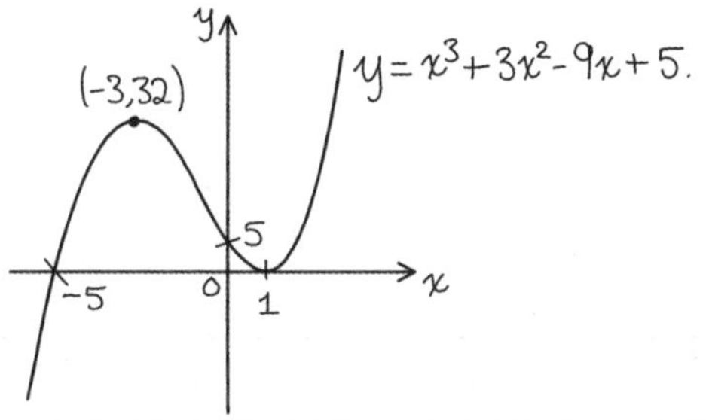

22

See **Exponentials and Logarithms** §5

$$\log_x 8 + \log_x 4 = 5$$
$$\log_x 32 = 5$$
$$x^5 = 32$$
$$x = \sqrt[5]{32}$$
$$= 2.$$

Remember:
- $\log_a u + \log_a v = \log_a uv$
- $\log_a u = v \Leftrightarrow a^v = u.$

23

See **Trigonometry** §4 and §5

$$\sin 2x - \cos x = 0$$
$$2\sin x\cos x - \cos x = 0$$
$$\cos x(2\sin x - 1) = 0$$

Using: $\sin 2A = 2\sin A\cos A$

$\cos x = 0$ or $2\sin x - 1 = 0$

$$\sin x = \frac{1}{2}$$

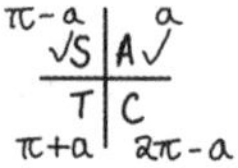

$$a = \sin^{-1}\left(\frac{1}{2}\right)$$
$$= \frac{\pi}{6}$$

Exact value...

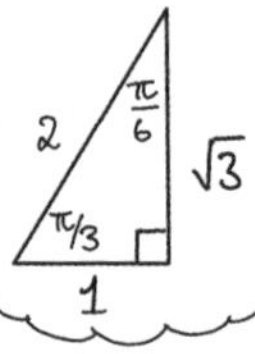

$$x = \frac{\pi}{2} \text{ or } \frac{3\pi}{2} \text{ or } \frac{\pi}{6} \text{ or } \frac{5\pi}{6}.$$

24

See **Trigonometry** §3 and §4

From the diagram: $D\hat{E}A = 2x + 90$.

So $\cos(D\hat{E}A^\circ) = \cos(2x^\circ + 90^\circ)$

$$= -\sin(2x^\circ)$$
$$= -2\sin x^\circ \cos x^\circ$$
$$= -2 \times \frac{1}{\sqrt{10}} \times \frac{3}{\sqrt{10}}$$
$$= -\frac{6}{10} = -\frac{3}{5}.$$

Remember: $\cos(u^\circ + 90^\circ) = -\sin u^\circ$.

Note: you could have used the addition formula.

By Pythagoras's Theorem:

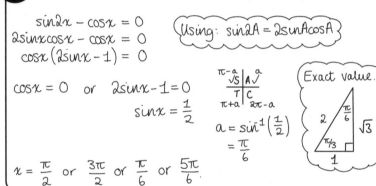

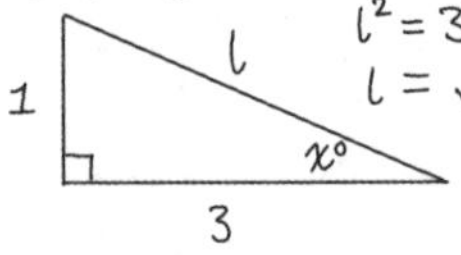

$$l^2 = 3^2 + 1^2$$
$$l = \sqrt{10}.$$

25

See **Integration** §3

$$f(x) = \int f'(x)\,dx$$
$$= \int 6x(x-2)\,dx$$
$$= \int (6x^2 - 12x)\,dx$$
$$= \frac{6x^3}{3} - \frac{12x^2}{2} + c$$
$$= 2x^3 - 6x^2 + c.$$

We know $f(1) = 4$, i.e. $2 \times 1^3 - 6 \times 1^2 + c = 4$
$$-4 + c = 4$$
$$c = 8.$$

So $f(x) = 2x^3 - 6x^2 + 8$.

2008 SQP Paper 2

1

See **Vectors** §12

$|\overrightarrow{QP}| = \sqrt{(-1)^2 + 3^2 + (-2)^2} = \sqrt{1+9+4} = \sqrt{14}$

$|\overrightarrow{QR}| = \sqrt{(-5)^2 + 1^2 + 1^2} = \sqrt{25+1+1} = \sqrt{27}$

$\overrightarrow{QP}.\overrightarrow{QR} = -1 \times (-5) + 3 \times 1 - 2 \times 1 = 5 + 3 - 2 = 6.$

$$\cos P\hat{Q}R = \frac{\overrightarrow{QP}.\overrightarrow{QR}}{|\overrightarrow{QP}||\overrightarrow{QR}|} = \frac{6}{\sqrt{14}\sqrt{27}}$$

Using: $\underline{a} . \underline{b} = |\underline{a}||\underline{b}|\cos\theta$

$$P\hat{Q}R = \cos^{-1}\left(\frac{6}{\sqrt{14}\sqrt{27}}\right)$$

$= 72.02°$ (to 2 d.p.)

<u>OR</u> 1.257 rads (to 3 d.p.)

2

See **Polynomials and Quadratics** §2

Given $2x^2 + px - 3 = 0$, let $a = 2$, $b = p$ and $c = -3$.

$$b^2 - 4ac = p^2 - 4 \times 2 \times (-3) = p^2 + 24.$$

But $p^2 \geq 0$ for all p, so $p^2 + 24 > 0$ for all p.

Hence the equation has real (and distinct) roots for all p.

3

See Differentiation §5

a

$$y = 6x^2 - x^3$$
$$\frac{dy}{dx} = 12x - 3x^2$$

Remember:
$$\frac{dy}{dx} = m_{tangent}.$$

Since the tangent at P has gradient 12:

$$12x - 3x^2 = 12$$
$$3x^2 - 12x + 12 = 0$$
$$x^2 - 4x + 4 = 0$$
$$(x-2)^2 = 0$$
$$x = 2.$$

b When $x = 2$, $y = 6 \times 2^2 - 2^3 = 24 - 8 = 16$. So P is $(2, 16)$.

The equation of the tangent is
$$y - 16 = 12(x-2)$$
$$y - 16 = 12x - 24$$
$$12x - y - 8 = 0.$$

4

See Wave Functions §5

a
$$3\cos x° + 5\sin x° = k\cos(x° - a°)$$
$$= k\cos x° \cos a° + k\sin x° \sin a°.$$
$$= (k\cos a°)\cos x° + (k\sin a°)\sin x°.$$

Comparing coefficients:
$$k\sin a° = 5$$
$$k\cos a° = 3$$

$$\frac{\checkmark S | A \checkmark\checkmark}{T | C \checkmark}$$

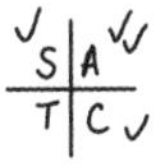

So $k = \sqrt{5^2 + 3^2}$ and $\tan a° = \dfrac{k\sin a°}{k\cos a°} = \dfrac{5}{3}$
$$= \sqrt{25 + 9}$$
$$= \sqrt{34}$$

$$a = \tan^{-1}\left(\frac{5}{3}\right) = 59.04 \text{ (to 2 d.p.)}$$

So $3\cos x° + 5\sin x° = \sqrt{34} \cos(x° - 59.04°)$.

cont...

b

$3\cos x° + 5\sin x° = 4$ $\quad\quad 0 \leq x \leq 90$

$\sqrt{34}\cos(x° - 59.04°) = 4$ $\quad\quad -59.04 \leq x - 59.04 \leq 30.96.^{*}$

$\cos(x° - 59.04°) = \dfrac{4}{\sqrt{34}}$

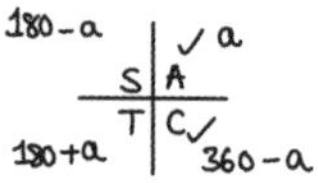

$a = \cos^{-1}\left(\dfrac{4}{\sqrt{34}}\right)$

$= 46.69$ (2 d.p.)

$x - 59.04 = 46.69$ or $360 - 46.69$

= ~~46.69~~ or ~~313.31~~

too large (see*)

Look 360° backwards:

$x - 59.04 = 46.69 - 360$ or $313.31 - 360$

= ~~-313.31~~ or -46.69

too small

So $x = -46.69 + 59.04$

$= 12.35.$

5

See **Differentiation** §11

a

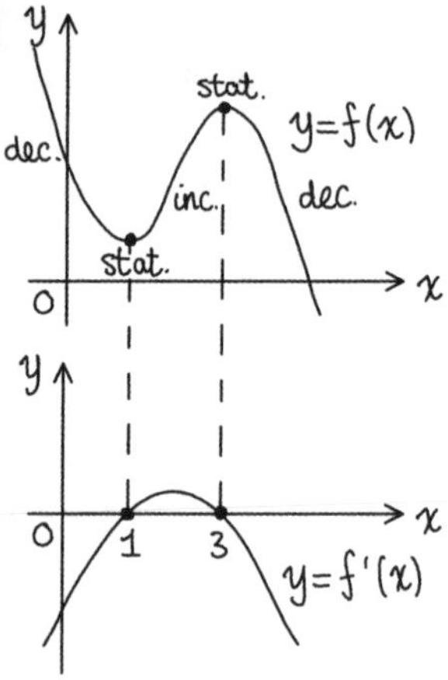

dec: $f(x)$ is decreasing so $f'(x) < 0$, i.e. $f'(x)$ is below the x-axis.

inc: $f(x)$ is increasing so $f'(x) > 0$, i.e. $f'(x)$ is above the x-axis.

stat: $f(x)$ is stationary so $f'(x) = 0$, i.e. $f'(x)$ lies on the x-axis.

6

(a) See **Circles** *§6 or §5*
(b) See **Circles** *§5*
(c) See **Straight Lines** *§1*

a Method 1

The centre is $A(6,1)$.

Using: $x^2+y^2+2gx+2fy+c=0$ has centre $(-g,-f)$.

$$m_{AP} = \frac{-1-1}{5-6} = \frac{-2}{-1} = 2.$$

So $m_{PT} = -\frac{1}{2}$ since the radius and tangent are perpendicular.

The equation of PT is:

$$y+1 = -\tfrac{1}{2}(x-5) \quad \text{using point } P(5,-1).$$
$$2y+2 = -(x-5) \quad \text{multiplying by 2.}$$
$$2y+2 = -x+5$$
$$x+2y = 3.$$

Method 2 Write $x+2y=3$ as $x=3-2y$ and substitute into the equation of the circle:

$$(3-2y)^2+y^2-12(3-2y)-2y+32=0$$
$$9-12y+4y^2+y^2-36+24y-2y+32=0$$
$$5y^2+10y+5=0$$
$$y^2+2y+1=0$$
$$(y+1)^2=0.$$

Since there is only one solution, the line is a tangent.
Check that P lies on the line: $x = 3-2\times(-1) = 5$.

cont...

2008 SQP

b Line PT has equation $x = 3 - 2y$. To find points of intersection, substitute this into the equation of the circle:

$$(3-2y)^2 + y^2 + 10(3-2y) + 2y + 6 = 0$$
$$9 - 12y + 4y^2 + y^2 + 30 - 20y + 2y + 6 = 0$$
$$5y^2 - 30y + 45 = 0$$
$$y^2 - 6y + 9 = 0$$
$$(y-3)^2 = 0$$
$$y = 3$$

You could also use the discriminant to show there is just one solution.

Since there is only one solution, the line is a tangent.

c When $y = 3$, $x = 3 - 2 \times 3 = -3$. So Q is the point $(-3, 3)$.

So $PQ = \sqrt{(-3-5)^2 + (3-(-1))^2}$

$= \sqrt{64+16}$

$= \sqrt{80}$

$= 4\sqrt{5}$

7

See **Differentiation** §12

a We are told that the surface area is 12 square units.

The surface area is given by:

$$2 \times \text{short side} + 2 \times \text{long side} + \text{base}$$
$$= 2 \times 2x \times h + 2 \times x \times h + 2x \times x$$
$$= 6xh + 2x^2 = 12$$

So $6xh = 12 - 2x^2$

$3xh = 6 - x^2$

$h = \dfrac{6-x^2}{3x}$.

The volume is $V(x) = 2x \times x \times h = 2x^2 . \dfrac{6-x^2}{3x} = \dfrac{2}{3}x(6-x^2)$.

cont...

b Stationary values exist where $V'(x)=0$.

$$V(x) = \tfrac{2}{3}x(6-x^2) = 4x - \tfrac{2}{3}x^3.$$

$$V'(x) = 4 - 2x^2 = 0$$

$$2x^2 = 4$$

$$x^2 = 2$$

$$x = \sqrt{2} \quad (\text{no "}\pm\text{" since lengths are positive})$$

Check this gives a maximum...

x	$\sqrt{2}^-$	$\sqrt{2}$	$\sqrt{2}^+$
$V'(x)$	+	0	–
Sketch	/	—	\

Hence the maximum volume occurs when $x = \sqrt{2}$.

8

See **Exponentials and Logarithms** §5

a We are told that $A_{1000} = 600$, i.e.:

$$A_0 e^{-0.002 \times 1000} = 600$$

$$A_0 e^{-2} = 600$$

$$A_0 = \frac{600}{e^{-2}}$$

$$= 600e^2$$

$$= 4433{\cdot}43 \text{ micrograms (to 2 d.p.)}$$

cont...

b

$$A_t = \frac{1}{2}A_0$$

$$A_0 e^{-0.002t} = \frac{1}{2}A_0$$

$$e^{-0.002t} = \frac{1}{2}$$

$$\log_e e^{-0.002t} = \log_e \frac{1}{2}$$ (taking $\log_e$ on both sides)

$$-0.002t = \log_e \frac{1}{2}$$

$$t = -\frac{\log_e \frac{1}{2}}{0.002}$$

$$= 346.57$$ years (to 2 d.p.)

Remember:
- $\log_a x^k = k\log_a x$
- $\log_a a = 1$.

9

See **Integration** §6

To find the limits of integration...

$$2x - \frac{1}{2}x^2 = 1.5$$

$$4x - x^2 = 3$$ multiplying through by 2.

$$x^2 - 4x + 3 = 0$$

$$(x-1)(x-3) = 0$$

$$x = 1 \text{ or } x = 3.$$

The shaded area is given by:

$$\int_1^3 (\text{upper} - \text{lower})\,dx = \int_1^3 \left(2x - \frac{1}{2}x^2 - 1.5\right)dx$$

$$= \left[x^2 - \frac{1}{6}x^3 - 1.5x\right]_1^3$$

$$= 9 - \frac{27}{6} - 4.5 - \left(1 - \frac{1}{6} - 1.5\right)$$

$$= \frac{2}{3}$$ square units.

2009 Paper 1

1

See **Sequences** §2

$u_2 = 3u_1 + 4 = 3 \times 2 + 4 = 10.$
$u_3 = 3u_2 + 4 = 3 \times 10 + 4 = 34.$

A

2

See **Circles** §3

Comparing with $x^2+y^2+2gx+2fy+c$,
$2g = 8$, $2f = 6$ and $c = -75$
$g = 4$ $f = 3$

The circle $x^2+y^2+2gx+2fy+c=0$ has radius $\sqrt{g^2+f^2-c}$.

The radius is $\sqrt{4^2+3^2+75} = \sqrt{16+9+75} = \sqrt{100} = 10.$

B

3

See **Straight Lines** §7

$S = \text{midpoint}_{QR} = \left(\frac{3-1}{2}, \frac{6-(4)}{2}\right) = (1, 5).$

So $m_{PS} = \frac{5-(-2)}{1-(-3)} = \frac{7}{4}.$

D

4

See **Differentiation** §5

$\frac{dy}{dx} = 15x^2 - 12.$

Remember: the derivative gives the gradient of the tangent.

When $x = 1$, the gradient of the tangent is $15 \times 1^2 - 12 = 3$

C

5

See **Straight Lines** §1 and §3

The length of ST is $\sqrt{(5-2)^2+(-1-3)^2} = \sqrt{3^2+4^2} = 5$ units

$m_{ST} = \frac{-1-3}{5-2} = -\frac{4}{3}.$

B

2009

6

See **Sequences** §4

Method 1 $l = \frac{b}{1-a}$ with $a = 0{\cdot}7$ and $b = 10$.

$$l = \frac{10}{1-0{\cdot}7} = \frac{10}{0{\cdot}3} = \frac{100}{3}.$$

Method 2 As $n \to \infty$, $u_{n+1} = u_n = l$

$$\begin{aligned} \text{So} \quad l &= 0{\cdot}7l + 10 \\ 0{\cdot}3l &= 10 \\ l &= \frac{10}{0{\cdot}3} = \frac{100}{3}. \end{aligned}$$

A

7

See **Trigonometry** §4

$$\begin{aligned} \cos 2x &= 2\cos^2 x - 1 \\ &= 2\left(\frac{1}{\sqrt{5}}\right)^2 - 1 \\ &= \frac{2}{5} - 1 \\ &= -\frac{3}{5}. \end{aligned}$$

Using: $\cos 2A = 2\cos^2 A - 1$

A

8

See **Differentiation** §2

$$\frac{1}{4x^3} = \frac{1}{4}x^{-3}.$$

So $\frac{d}{dx}\left(\frac{1}{4x^3}\right) = \frac{d}{dx}\left(\frac{1}{4}x^{-3}\right) = -\frac{3}{4}x^{-4} = -\frac{3}{4x^4}.$

D

9

See **Circles** §4

Put $y = 2x$ in the equation of the circle:

$$\begin{aligned} x^2 + (2x)^2 &= 5 \\ x^2 + 4x^2 &= 5 \\ 5x^2 &= 5 \\ x^2 &= 1 \\ x &= \pm 1. \end{aligned}$$

A

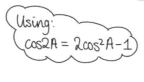

10

See **Functions and Graphs** §6 and §10 or **Exponentials and Logarithms** §7

<u>Method 1</u> The curve $y = \log_5 x$ has graph

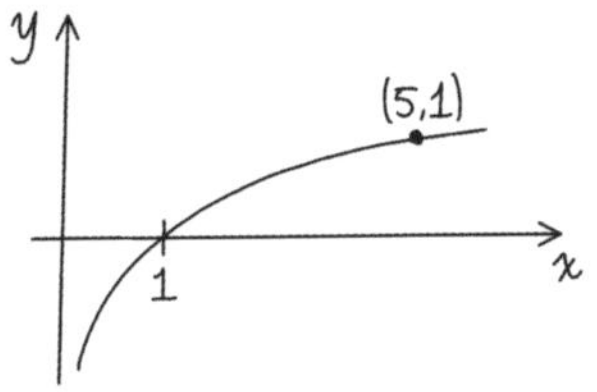

and $y = \log_5(x-2)$ is this shifted 2 units to the right.

<u>Method 2</u> When $y = 0$, $\log_5(x-2) = 0$

$$x - 2 = 5^0$$

$$x = 3.$$

So the curve passes through $(3, 0)$.

B

11

See **Trigonometry** §1

$(4\sin x - \sqrt{5})(\sin x + 1) = 0$

$4\sin x - \sqrt{5} = 0$ or $\sin x + 1 = 0$

$\sin x = \frac{\sqrt{5}}{4}$ $\quad$ $\sin x = -1$ ← One solution

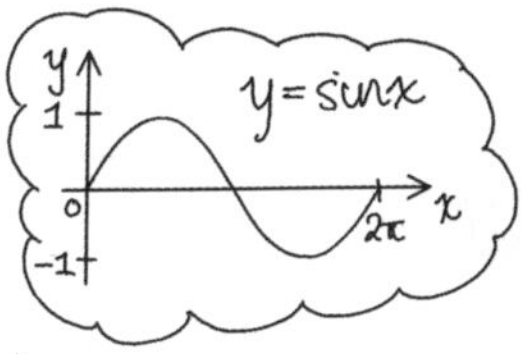

Since $\frac{\sqrt{5}}{4} < 1$ this part has two solutions in $0 \leq x < 2\pi$

Therefore there are 3 solutions in $0 \leq x < 2\pi$.

B

2009

12

See **Polynomials and Quadratics** §2

Let $a = 2$, $b = -1$ and $c = -9$, then the discriminant is

$$b^2 - 4ac = (-1)^2 - 4 \times 2 \times (-9) = 1 + 72 = 73.$$

Since $b^2 - 4ac > 0$, the roots are real and distinct, and because 73 is not a square number, the roots are not rational.

C

13

See **Wave Functions** §1

$k\sin a^\circ = 1$
$k\cos a^\circ = \sqrt{3}$

So $k = \sqrt{1^2 + \sqrt{3}^2}$
$= \sqrt{4}$
$= 2$

and $\tan a^\circ = \dfrac{k\sin a^\circ}{k\cos a^\circ} = \dfrac{1}{\sqrt{3}}$

$a = \tan^{-1}\left(\dfrac{1}{\sqrt{3}}\right)$
$= 30.$

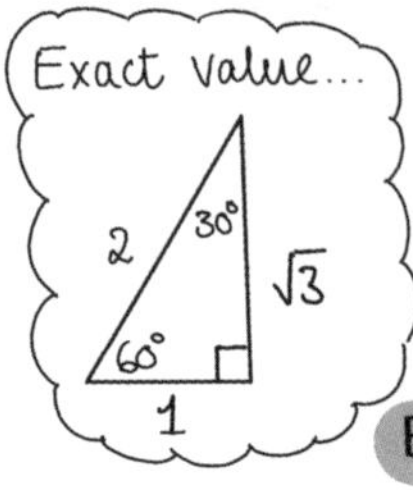

B

14

See **Functions and Graphs** §9 and §10

$f(x) = 2\sin\left(3x - \frac{\pi}{2}\right) + 5$

Scales the graph to have amplitude 2

Shifts the graph 5 units up the y-axis.

So the range is $3 \leq f(x) \leq 7$.

C

15

See **Straight Lines** §3

The line makes an angle of $\frac{\pi}{2} - \frac{\pi}{6} = \frac{\pi}{3}$ with the positive direction of the x-axis.

So the gradient is $\tan\frac{\pi}{3} = \sqrt{3}$.

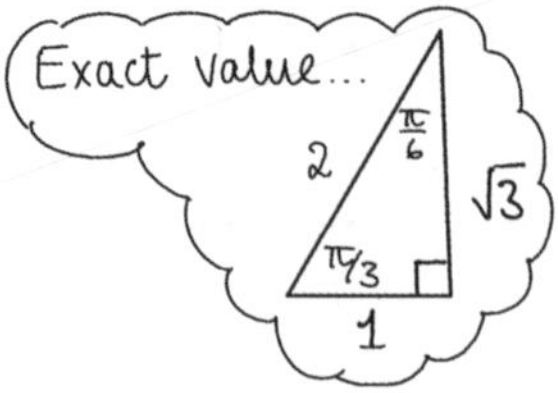

A

16

See **Integration** §5

Since the shaded region lies below the x-axis, its area is given by

$$-\int_0^1 (4x^3 - 9x^2)\,dx = -\left[x^4 - 3x^3\right]_0^1.$$

B

17

See **Vectors** §3

$$|\underline{u}| = \sqrt{(-3)^2 + 4^2} = \sqrt{25} = 5.$$

So $\frac{1}{5}\underline{u}$ is a unit vector parallel to $\underline{u}$.

$$\frac{1}{5}\underline{u} = \begin{pmatrix} -3/5 \\ 0 \\ 4/5 \end{pmatrix} = -\frac{3}{5}\underline{i} + \frac{4}{5}\underline{k}.$$

A

18

See **Further Calculus** §4

Using the chain rule,

$$f'(x) = -\frac{1}{2}\left(4 - 3x^2\right)^{-3/2} \times \frac{d}{dx}\left(4 - 3x^2\right)$$

$$= -\frac{1}{2}\left(4 - 3x^2\right)^{-3/2} \times (-6x)$$

$$= 3x\left(4 - 3x^2\right)^{-3/2}.$$

D

19

See **Polynomials and Quadratics** §6

$$6 + x - x^2 < 0$$

$$-\left(x^2 - x - 6\right) < 0$$

$$-(x+2)(x-3) < 0$$

Sketch:

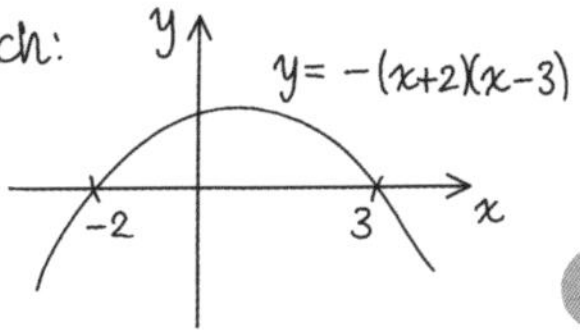

From the sketch, $x < -2$ or $x > 3$.

C

20

See **Differentiation** §4

$$\frac{dA}{dr} = 4\pi r + 6\pi.$$

When $r = 2$, $\frac{dA}{dr} = 8\pi + 6\pi = 14\pi$.

Remember: "rate of change" means "derivative".

C

21

See **Straight Lines** – (*a*) §6, (*b*) §8, (*c*) §6 and §10

a Put $y = 0$ in the equation of PQ:

$$6x - 7 \times 0 + 18 = 0$$
$$6x = -18$$
$$x = -3.$$ So P has coordinates $(-3, 0)$.

b $m_{QR} = \dfrac{-2-6}{8-4} = \dfrac{-8}{4} = -2$. So $m_{alt.} = \dfrac{1}{2}$ since $m_{QR} \times m_{alt.} = -1$.

So the equation is $y = \frac{1}{2}(x+3)$ using point $P(-3,0)$

$$2y = x + 3$$

c We know $m_{QR} = -2$.

So the equation of QR is $y - 6 = -2(x-4)$ using point $Q(4,6)$.

$$y - 6 = -2x + 8$$
$$y = -2x + 14.$$

Solve the equations of QR and PT simultaneously...

$$2y = x + 3 \quad \text{——— ①}$$
$$y = -2x + 14 \quad \text{—— ②}$$

② + 2×①: $5y = 20$

$$y = 4$$

When $y = 4$, $x = 2 \times 4 - 3 = 5$. So T is the point $(5, 4)$.

2009

22

See **Vectors** – *(a) §9 and §10, (b) §13*

a i $\overrightarrow{DE} = \underline{e} - \underline{d} = \begin{pmatrix} 1 \\ -2 \\ -3 \end{pmatrix} - \begin{pmatrix} 10 \\ -8 \\ -15 \end{pmatrix} = \begin{pmatrix} -9 \\ 6 \\ 12 \end{pmatrix} = 3\begin{pmatrix} -3 \\ 2 \\ 4 \end{pmatrix}$

$\overrightarrow{EF} = \underline{f} - \underline{e} = \begin{pmatrix} -2 \\ 0 \\ 1 \end{pmatrix} - \begin{pmatrix} 1 \\ -2 \\ -3 \end{pmatrix} = \begin{pmatrix} -3 \\ 2 \\ 4 \end{pmatrix}$

$\overrightarrow{EF}$ and $\overrightarrow{DE}$ have a common point and, since $3\overrightarrow{EF} = \overrightarrow{DE}$, they have a common direction. Hence D, E and F are collinear.

ii Since $3\overrightarrow{EF} = \overrightarrow{DE}$, E divides DF in the ratio 3 : 1.

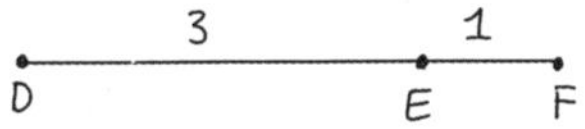

b $\overrightarrow{GE} = \underline{e} - \underline{g} = \begin{pmatrix} 1 \\ -2 \\ -3 \end{pmatrix} - \begin{pmatrix} k \\ 1 \\ 0 \end{pmatrix} = \begin{pmatrix} 1-k \\ -3 \\ -3 \end{pmatrix}$.

Since DE and GE are perpendicular, $\overrightarrow{DE}.\overrightarrow{GE} = 0$. So

$$-9(1-k) + 6\times(-3) + 12\times(-3) = 0$$
$$-9 + 9k - 18 - 36 = 0$$
$$9k = 63$$
$$k = 7.$$

23

See **Functions and Graphs** §10

a

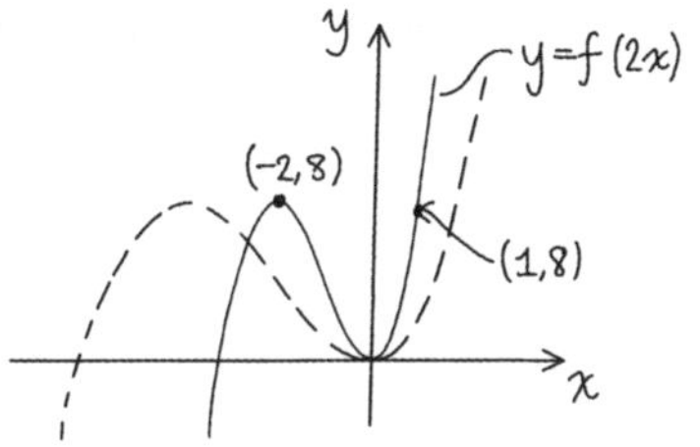

$y = f(2x)$ multiplies each x-coordinate by $\frac{1}{2}$.

b $y = 1 - f(2x) = -f(2x) + 1$.

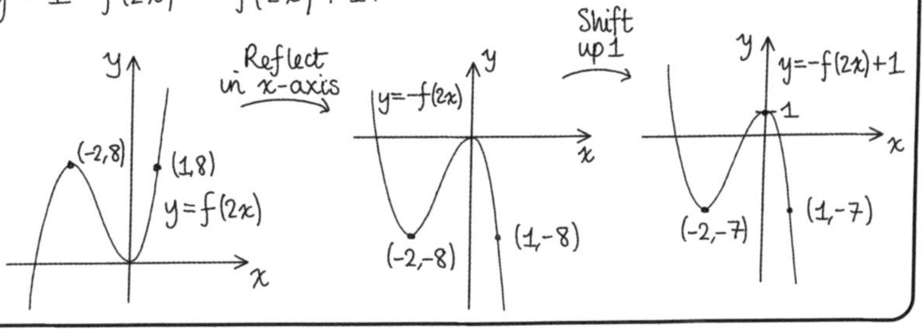

2009

24

See **Trigonometry** §3

a $\sin\left(\frac{7\pi}{12}\right) = \sin\left(\frac{\pi}{3}+\frac{\pi}{4}\right) = \sin\frac{\pi}{3}\cos\frac{\pi}{4} + \cos\frac{\pi}{3}\sin\frac{\pi}{4}$

$$= \frac{\sqrt{3}}{2} \times \frac{1}{\sqrt{2}} + \frac{1}{2} \times \frac{1}{\sqrt{2}}$$

$$= \frac{\sqrt{3}+1}{2\sqrt{2}}.$$

Using:
$\sin(A+B)$
$= \sin A\cos B + \cos A\sin B$

b $\sin(A+B) = \sin A\cos B + \cos A\sin B$
$\sin(A-B) = \sin A\cos B - \cos A\sin B$

Adding gives $\sin(A+B) + \sin(A-B) = 2\sin A\cos B$.

c **i** $\frac{\pi}{12} = \frac{\pi}{3} - \frac{\pi}{4}$

ii Since $\frac{7\pi}{12} = \frac{\pi}{3} + \frac{\pi}{4}$ and $\frac{\pi}{12} = \frac{\pi}{3} - \frac{\pi}{4}$, use the above formula with $A = \frac{\pi}{3}$ and $B = \frac{\pi}{4}$.

$$\sin\left(\frac{7\pi}{12}\right) + \sin\left(\frac{\pi}{12}\right) = 2\sin\frac{\pi}{3}\cos\frac{\pi}{4}$$

$$= 2 \times \frac{\sqrt{3}}{2} \times \frac{1}{\sqrt{2}}$$

$$= \frac{\sqrt{3}}{\sqrt{2}} = \frac{\sqrt{6}}{2}$$

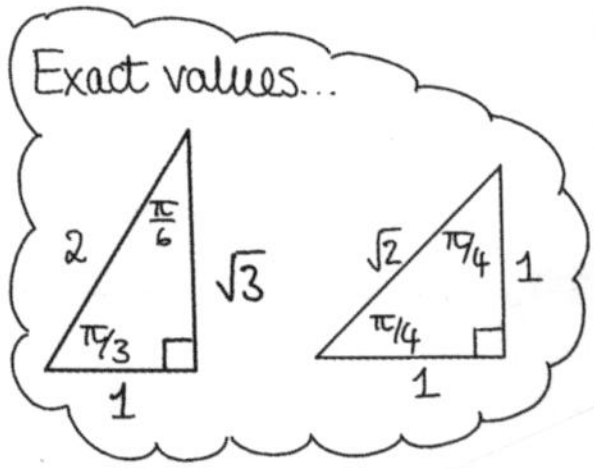

2009

2009 Paper 2

1

See **Differentiation** §7 and §8

Stationary points exist where $\frac{dy}{dx} = 0$.

$$\frac{dy}{dx} = 3x^2 - 6x - 9 = 0$$
$$3(x^2 - 2x - 3) = 0$$
$$(x+1)(x-3) = 0$$
$$x = -1, \quad x = 3.$$

When $x = -1$, $y = (-1)^3 - 3\times(-1)^2 - 9\times(-1) + 12$
$= -1 - 3 + 9 + 12$
$= 17.$ $\quad (-1, 17)$.

When $x = 3$, $y = 3^3 - 3\times 3^2 - 9\times 3 + 12$
$= -15.$ $\quad (3, -15)$.

Method 1 Nature table:

x	-1^-	-1	-1^+	3^-	3	3^+
dy/dx	+	0	−	−	0	+
Sketch	/	—	\	\	_	/

Method 2 Second derivative test: $\frac{d^2y}{dx^2} = 6x - 6$.

When $x = -1$, $\frac{d^2y}{dx^2} = 6\times(-1) - 6 = -12 < 0$

When $x = 3$, $\frac{d^2y}{dx^2} = 6\times 3 - 6 = 12 > 0$.

So $(-1, 17)$ is a maximum turning point.
$(3, -15)$ is a minimum turning point.

2009

2

(a) See **Functions and Graphs** §3
(b) See **Differentiation** §2

a i $p(x) = f(g(x)) = f(x^2-2) = 3(x^2-2)+1 = 3x^2-5.$

ii $q(x) = g(f(x)) = g(3x+1) = (3x+1)^2-2.$

b $p'(x) = 6x$ and $q'(x) = 2(3x+1) \times \frac{d}{dx}(3x+1) = 6(3x+1).$

So
$$6x = 6(3x+1)$$
$$x = 3x+1$$
$$2x = -1$$
$$x = -\frac{1}{2}.$$

3

(a) See **Polynomials and Quadratics** §9
(b) See **Exponentials and Logarithms** §3 and §5

a i **Method 1** Put $x=1$ in the left-hand side:

$$1^3+8\times1^2+11\times1-20 = 1+8+11-20 = 0.$$

So $x=1$ is a root of the equation.

Method 2 Using synthetic division...

1	1	8	11	−20
		1	9	20
	1	9	20	0

Since the remainder is 0, $x=1$ is a root.

ii $x^3+8x^2+11x-20 = (x-1)(x^2+9x+20)$ ← By inspection or from the table.
$= (x-1)(x+4)(x+5).$

cont...

b $\log_2(x+3) + \log_2(x^2+5x-4) = 3$

$\log_2((x+3)(x^2+5x-4)) = 3$

$(x+3)(x^2+5x-4) = 2^3$

$x^3 + 8x^2 + 11x - 12 = 8$

$x^3 + 8x^2 + 11x - 20 = 0$

$(x-1)(x+4)(x+5) = 0$

So $x = 1$, $x = -4$, $x = -5$

Remember:
- $\log_a x + \log_a y = \log_a xy$
- $\log_a x = y \Leftrightarrow x = a^y$.

Remember: we can only take log of a positive number.

But when $x = -4$, $\log_2(x+3) = \log_2(-1)$ which is undefined.

$x = -5$, $\log_2(x+3) = \log_2(-2)$ which is undefined.

So the only solution is $x = 1$.

4

(a) See **Circles** *§2*
(b) See **Straight LInes** *§2 and* **Circles** *§6*
(c) See **Circles** *§7*

a Put $x = 5$ and $y = 10$ in the left-hand side:

$(5+1)^2 + (10-2)^2 = 36 + 64 = 100$.

Since this equals the right-hand side, P lies on the circle.

b The circle has centre $C(-1, 2)$.

The circle $(x-a)^2 + (y-b)^2 = r^2$ has centre (a, b).

Let Q have coordinates (x_Q, y_Q). Since C is the midpoint of PQ,

$$(-1, 2) = \left(\frac{x_Q + 5}{2}, \frac{y_Q + 10}{2}\right).$$

So $x_Q + 5 = -2$ and $y_Q + 10 = 4$

$x_Q = -7$ $\quad$ $y_Q = -6$.

Hence Q is the point $(-7, -6)$.

Now $m_{PQ} = m_{CP} = \frac{10-2}{5-(-1)} = \frac{8}{6} = \frac{4}{3}$,

so $m_{tgt.} = -\frac{3}{4}$ since $m_{PQ} \times m_{tgt.} = -1$.

cont...

Therefore the equation of the tangent at Q is

$$y+6=-\tfrac{3}{4}(x+7) \quad \text{using } Q(-7,-6).$$

$$4y+24=-3x-21$$

$$3x+4y+45=0.$$

c Circle C_1 has radius 10.
So the radii of C_2 and C_3 are both 20.

The circle $(x-a)^2+(y-b)^2=r^2$ has radius r.

The point $P(5,10)$ is the centre of C_2, so the equation of C_2 is

$$(x-5)^2+(y-10)^2=20^2$$

i.e. $(x-5)^2+(y-10)^2=400.$

Sketch:

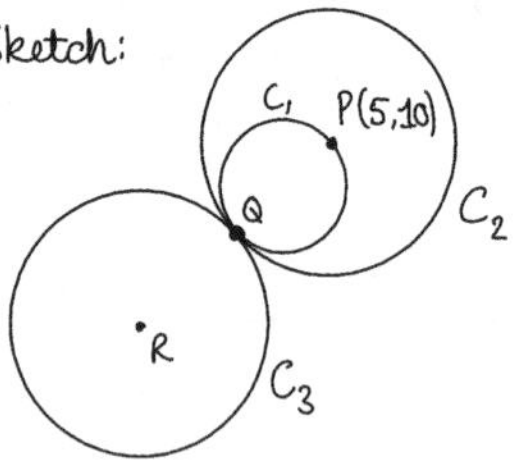

The point Q is the midpoint of PR, so

$$\left(\frac{5+x_R}{2}, \frac{10+y_R}{2}\right)=(-7,-6)$$

i.e. $\dfrac{5+x_R}{2}=-7$ and $\dfrac{10+y_R}{2}=-6$

$x_R=-19.$ $\qquad y_R=-22.$

So R is the point $(-19,-22)$ and C_3 has equation

$$(x+19)^2+(y+22)^2=400.$$

5

(a) See **Functions and Graphs** §9
(b) See **Trigonometry** §1
(c) See **Integration** §6

a The period of $g(x)$ is π, so $n = 2$. The amplitude is 3 so $m = 3$.

b The curves intersect where

$$-4\cos 2x + 3 = 3\cos 2x$$
$$7\cos 2x = 3$$
$$\cos 2x = \frac{3}{7}.$$

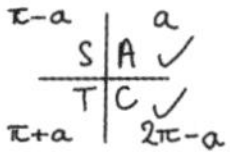

$$a = \cos^{-1}\left(\frac{3}{7}\right)$$
$$= 1.128 \text{ (to 3 d.p.)}$$

So $2x = 1.128$ or $2x = 2\pi - 1.128$

$x = 0.564$ $\quad$ $x = 2.578$ (to 3 d.p.)

When $x = 0.564$, $y = 3\cos(2 \times 0.564)$
$= 1.285.$

When $x = 2.578$, $y = 3\cos(2 \times 2.578)$
$= 1.288.$ (both to 3 d.p.)

To get a more accurate answer, we can work to 3 d.p. and round at the end.

So the points of intersection are $(0.6, 1.3)$ and $(2.6, 1.3)$ to 1 d.p.

c The shaded area is

$$\int_{0.6}^{2.6} (\text{upper} - \text{lower})\, dx$$
$$= \int_{0.6}^{2.6} (-4\cos 2x + 3 - 3\cos 2x)\, dx$$
$$= \int_{0.6}^{2.6} (-7\cos 2x + 3)\, dx$$
$$= \left[-\frac{7}{2}\sin 2x + 3x\right]_{0.6}^{2.6}$$
$$= 10.89 + 1.46$$
$$= 12.4 \text{ square units (to 1 d.p.)}$$

Using: $\int \cos ax\, dx = \frac{1}{a}\sin ax + c$.

6

See **Exponentials and Logarithms** §5

a Let N be the population in millions.

- The rate of increase is $1.6\% = 0.016$. So $r = 0.016$.
- 2020 is 14 years after 2006, so $t = 14$.

$N = N_0 e^{rt} = 61e^{0.016 \times 14} = 76.32$ (to 2 d.p.)

So the population would be 76.32 million.

b This time, $r = 0.43\% = 0.0043$.

For the population to double, $N = 2N_0$ so

$$N = N_0 e^{0.0043t}$$
$$2N_0 = N_0 e^{0.0043t}$$
$$e^{0.0043t} = 2$$
$$0.0043t = \log_e 2$$
$$t = \frac{\log_e 2}{0.0043}$$
$$t = 161.20 \text{ (to 2 d.p.)}$$

Remember: $a^y = x \Leftrightarrow y = \log_a x$

So the population would take 161.20 years to double.

2009

7

See **Vectors** – (a) §14 and §11, (b) §5 and §3

a

$$\underset{\sim}{p}\cdot(\underset{\sim}{q}+\underset{\sim}{r}) = \underset{\sim}{p}\cdot\underset{\sim}{q} + \underset{\sim}{p}\cdot\underset{\sim}{r}$$
$$= |\underset{\sim}{p}||\underset{\sim}{q}|\cos 30^\circ + 0$$ ← since $\underset{\sim}{p}$ and $\underset{\sim}{r}$ are perpendicular.
$$= 4\times 3\times \cos 30^\circ$$
$$= 4\times 3\times \frac{\sqrt{3}}{2}$$
$$= 6\sqrt{3}.$$

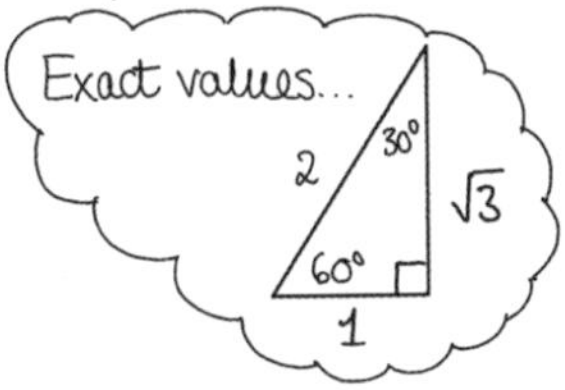

$$\underset{\sim}{r}\cdot(\underset{\sim}{p}-\underset{\sim}{q}) = \underset{\sim}{r}\cdot\underset{\sim}{p} - \underset{\sim}{r}\cdot\underset{\sim}{q}$$
$$= 0 - |\underset{\sim}{r}||\underset{\sim}{q}|\cos\theta$$
$$= -\frac{3}{2}\times 3\times(-\cos 60^\circ)$$
$$= \frac{3}{2}\times 3\times\frac{1}{2}$$
$$= \frac{9}{4}.$$

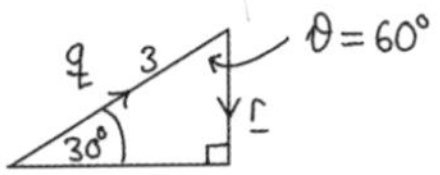

$$|\underset{\sim}{r}| = 3\sin 30^\circ = \frac{3}{2}.$$

b

From the diagram, $\underset{\sim}{q}+\underset{\sim}{r} = \overrightarrow{DE}$
and $\underset{\sim}{p}-\underset{\sim}{q} = -\underset{\sim}{q}+\underset{\sim}{p} = \overrightarrow{AC}$

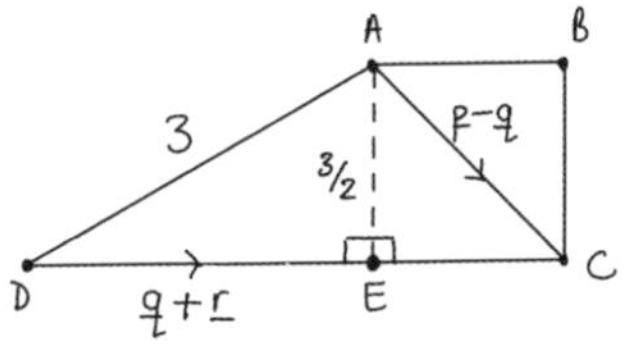

Using Pythagoras's theorem:

$$|\underset{\sim}{q}+\underset{\sim}{r}| = \sqrt{3^2-(3/2)^2} = \sqrt{\frac{27}{4}} = \frac{\sqrt{9}\sqrt{3}}{\sqrt{4}} = \frac{3\sqrt{3}}{2} \quad (= 2.60 \text{ to } 2\text{ d.p.})$$

Now $|EC| = |\underset{\sim}{p}| - \frac{3\sqrt{3}}{2} = 4 - \frac{3\sqrt{3}}{2}$

So $|\underset{\sim}{p}-\underset{\sim}{q}| = \sqrt{\left(4-\frac{3\sqrt{3}}{2}\right)^2+\left(\frac{3}{2}\right)^2} = \sqrt{25-12\sqrt{3}} \quad (= 2.05 \text{ to } 2\text{ d.p.})$

2009

2010 Paper 1

1

See **Straight Lines** §5 and §6

To extract the gradient, rearrange to give $y = mx + c$...

$$2x - 3y - 6 = 0$$
$$3y = 2x - 6$$
$$y = \frac{2}{3}x - 2$$

So this line has gradient $\frac{2}{3}$.

Therefore L has gradient $-\frac{3}{2}$ since $m \times m_{\perp} = -1$.

A

2

See **Sequences** §2

$$u_1 = 2u_0 + 3 = 2 \times 1 + 3 = 5$$
$$u_2 = 2u_1 + 3 = 2 \times 5 + 3 = 13$$

C

3

See **Vectors** §5 and §6

$$3\underline{u} - 2\underline{v} = 3\begin{pmatrix}2\\0\\1\end{pmatrix} - 2\begin{pmatrix}-1\\2\\4\end{pmatrix} = \begin{pmatrix}6\\0\\3\end{pmatrix} - \begin{pmatrix}-2\\4\\8\end{pmatrix} = \begin{pmatrix}8\\-4\\-5\end{pmatrix}$$

D

2010

4

See **Functions and Graphs** §9 and §10

The amplitude (height) is 2 so $a = 2$.

The period is $\frac{2\pi}{3}$ so $b = 3$.

A

5

See **Polynomials and Quadratics** §3

__Method 1__ Compensating...

$$x^2 + 8x + 3 = (x+4)^2 - 16 + 3 = (x+4)^2 - 13. \text{ So } q = -13.$$

(This gives the correct x^2 and x terms, and an extra 16)

(Take off this extra 16)

cont...

Method 2 Comparing coefficients...

$$x^2 + 8x + 3 = (x+p)^2 + q$$
$$= x^2 + 2px + p^2 + q.$$

So $2p = 8$ and $p^2 + q = 3$
$p = 4$ $\quad q = 3 - 16$
$= -13.$

B

6

See **Polynomials and Quadratics** §2

Given $kx^2 - 3x + 2 = 0$, let $a = k$, $b = -3$ and $c = 2$.

For equal roots, $b^2 - 4ac = 0$ i.e.

$$(-3)^2 - 4 \times k \times 2 = 0$$
$$8k = 9$$
$$k = \frac{9}{8}.$$

D

7

See **Sequences** §4

Method 1 $l = \frac{b}{1-a}$ with $a = \frac{1}{4}$ and $b = 7$.

$$l = \frac{7}{1 - 1/4} = \frac{7}{3/4} = \frac{28}{3}.$$

Method 2 As $n \to \infty$, $u_{n+1} = u_n = l$

So $l = \frac{1}{4}l + 7$
$\frac{3}{4}l = 7$
$l = \frac{28}{3}.$

C

8

See **Circles** §3

Comparing with $x^2 + y^2 + 2gx + 2fy + c$,
$2g = -6$ $\quad 2f = -10$ and $c = 9$
$g = -3$ $\quad f = -5$

The circle $x^2 + y^2 + 2gx + 2fy + c = 0$ has centre $(-g, -f)$.

The centre is $(3, 5)$. So l has equation $y = 10$.

B

9

See **Integration** §1 and **Further Calculus** §2

$$\int\left(2x^{-4} + \cos 5x\right) dx$$

$$= \frac{2x^{-3}}{-3} + \frac{1}{5}\sin 5x + c$$

$$= -\frac{2}{3}x^{-3} + \frac{1}{5}\sin 5x + c.$$

Using: $\int \cos ax \, dx = \frac{1}{a}\sin ax + c.$

C

10

See **Vectors** §13

The vectors are perpendicular ⇔ their scalar product is zero.

$$(x\underline{i} + 5\underline{j} + 7\underline{k}).(-3\underline{i} + 2\underline{j} - \underline{k}) = 0$$

$$x \times (-3) + 5 \times 2 + 7 \times (-1) = 0$$

$$-3x + 3 = 0$$

$$x = 1.$$

B

11

See **Functions and Graphs** §3 and §8

$$f\left(g\left(\tfrac{\pi}{6}\right)\right) = f\left(\tfrac{\pi}{6} + \tfrac{\pi}{6}\right)$$

$$= f\left(\tfrac{\pi}{3}\right)$$

$$= \cos\frac{\pi}{3}$$

$$= \frac{1}{2}.$$

Exact values...

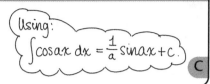

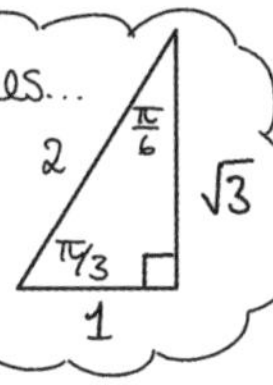

D

12

See **Differentiation** §2

$f(x) = x^{-1/5}$. So $f'(x) = -\frac{1}{5}x^{-6/5}$.

A

2010

13

See **Polynomials and Quadratics** §1 and §2

- $a > 0$ means the parabola is concave up (U-shaped)
- $b^2 - 4ac > 0$ means the parabola intersects the x-axis at two distinct points.

B

14

See **Integration** §6

The shaded area between $x = -2$ and $x = 2$ is given by

$$\int_{-2}^{2} (\text{upper} - \text{lower})\,dx = \int_{-2}^{2} \left(14 - x^2 - (2x^2 + 2)\right) dx$$
$$= \int_{-2}^{2} \left(12 - 3x^2\right) dx$$

C

2010

15

See **Differentiation** §6 and §7

At $x = 1$, $f'(1) = 1^2 - 9 = -8 < 0$. So the function is decreasing.
At $x = -3$, $f'(-3) = (-3)^2 - 9 = 0$. So the function is stationary.

C

16

See **Polynomials and Quadratics** §12

The curve intersects the x-axis where

$k(x-1)^2(x+t) = 0$.

ie $x = 1$ and $x = -t$.

Hence $-t = 5$ ie $t = -5$.

When $x = 0$, $y = k(-1)^2(-5) = 10$. So $k = -2$.

A

17

See **Differentiation** §4

$s(t) = t^2 - 5t + 8$

$s'(t) = 2t - 5$

$s'(3) = 2 \times 3 - 5 = 1.$

Remember: "rate of change" means "derivative".

B

18

See **Polynomials and Quadratics** §6

$x^2 + 4x > 0$

$x(x+4) > 0$

From the sketch, $x < -4$ or $x > 0$.

Sketch:

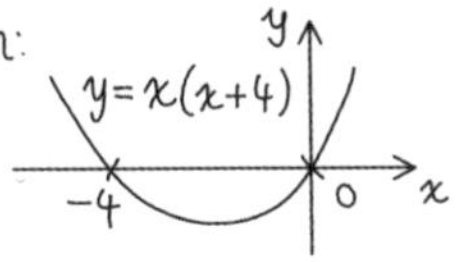

B

19

See **Exponentials and Logarithms** §7

The points (4,0) and (6,1) both lie on the curve.

So $\log_a(4+b) = 0$ and $\log_a(6+b) = 1$.

$\log_a(4+b) = 0 \Leftrightarrow a^0 = 4 + b$ ie $b = -3$

Then $\log_a 3 = 1 \Leftrightarrow a^1 = 3$ ie $a = 3$.

C

20

See **Functions and Graphs** §10

Method 1 Since (6,4) lies on $y = f(2x) - 3$,

$4 = f(2 \times 6) - 3$ ie $f(12) = 7$.

So $y = f(x)$ has turning point (12,7).

Method 2 Points on the curve $y = f(2x) - 3$ are points on $y = f(x)$ with the x-coordinates halved, and then shifted down by 3.

So to see where (6,4) came from, reverse this:

$(6 \times 2, 4 + 3) = (12, 7)$.

A

21

(a) See **Straight Lines** *§7*
(b) See **Straight Lines** *§6*
(c) See **Vectors** *§10*

a $\text{midpoint}_{AC} = \left(\frac{4+18}{2}, \frac{0+20}{2}\right) = (11,10)$. So $Q(11,10)$.

$m_{BQ} = \frac{10-16}{11-(-4)} = -\frac{6}{15} = -\frac{2}{5}$

So the equation of BQ is

$$y - 16 = -\frac{2}{5}(x-(-4)) \text{ using } B(-4,16)$$
$$5y - 80 = -2x - 8$$
$$2x + 5y - 72 = 0. \quad \text{——} \quad (*)$$

b Put $x = 6$ and $y = 12$ in the LHS of $(*)$:

$$2\times6 + 5\times12 - 72 = 12 + 60 - 72 = 0 = \text{RHS}$$

So T lies on BQ.

c $\overrightarrow{BT} = \underline{t} - \underline{b} = \begin{pmatrix}6\\12\end{pmatrix} - \begin{pmatrix}-4\\16\end{pmatrix} = \begin{pmatrix}10\\-4\end{pmatrix} = 2\begin{pmatrix}5\\-2\end{pmatrix}$.

$\overrightarrow{TQ} = \underline{q} - \underline{t} = \begin{pmatrix}11\\10\end{pmatrix} - \begin{pmatrix}6\\12\end{pmatrix} = \begin{pmatrix}5\\-2\end{pmatrix}$

So $2\overrightarrow{TQ} = \overrightarrow{BT}$ ie $\frac{BT}{TQ} = \frac{2}{1}$

So T divides BQ in the ratio $2:1$.

22

See **Polynomials and Quadratics** – (a) and (b) §9, (c) and (d) §7 and §11

a i $x-1$ is a factor $\Leftrightarrow f(1)=0$.

Method 1 $f(1) = 2\times1^3+1^2-8\times1+5 = 2+1-8+5=0$.

Method 2 Using synthetic division...

$$\begin{array}{c|cccc} 1 & 2 & 1 & -8 & 5 \\ & & 2 & 3 & -5 \\ \hline & 2 & 3 & -5 & \boxed{0} \end{array}$$

Since $f(1)=0$, $x-1$ is a factor of $f(x)$.

ii
$$\begin{aligned} f(x) &= 2x^3+x^2-8x+5 \\ &= (x-1)(2x^2+3x-5) \\ &= (x-1)(2x+5)(x-1) \\ &= (x-1)^2(2x+5). \end{aligned}$$

By inspection or from the table.

b
$$\begin{aligned} 2x^3+x^2-8x+5 &= 0 \\ (x-1)^2(2x+5) &= 0 \\ x = 1 \quad &\text{or} \quad x=-\frac{5}{2} \end{aligned}$$

c Equate to find the points of intersection ...

$$\begin{aligned} 2x^3+x^2-6x+2 &= 2x-3 \\ 2x^3+x^2-8x+5 &= 0 \\ (x-1)^2(2x+5) &= 0 \\ x = 1 \quad &\text{or} \quad x=-\frac{5}{2} \end{aligned}$$

From above

Since $x=1$ is a repeated root, the line is a tangent to the curve at the point where $x=1$.

At $x=1$, $y=2\times1-3=-1$. So $G(1,-1)$.

d The other point of intersection has $x=-\frac{5}{2}$.

At $x=-\frac{5}{2}$, $y=2\times\left(-\frac{5}{2}\right)-3=-8$. So $H\left(-\frac{5}{2},-8\right)$.

2010

23

(a) and (b) See **Straight Lines** *§3 and §6, and* **Trigonometry** *§3*
(c) See **Trigonometry** *§3*

a i To extract the gradient of OA, rearrange to the form $y = mx + c$...

$$3x - 2y = 0 \quad \text{i.e.} \quad y = \frac{3}{2}x$$

So the gradient m is $\frac{3}{2}$.

Hence $\tan a = \frac{3}{2}$.

> Remember: the line $y = mx + c$ has $m = \tan\theta$ where θ is the angle between the line and the positive direction of the x-axis.

ii $\tan a = \frac{\text{opp.}}{\text{adj.}} = \frac{3}{2}$. So we have:

> By Pythagoras's theorem.

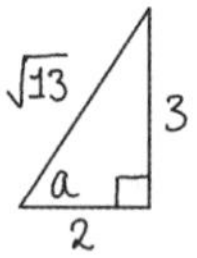

So $\sin a = \frac{\text{opp.}}{\text{hyp.}} = \frac{3}{\sqrt{13}}$.

b $3x - 4y = 0 \Leftrightarrow y = \frac{3}{4}x$. So OB has gradient $\frac{3}{4}$.

Hence $\tan b = \frac{3}{4}$, so we have:

> By Pythagoras's theorem.

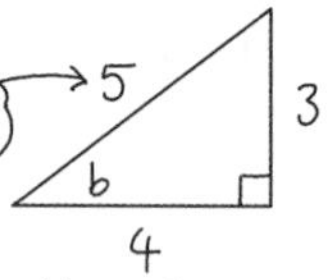

So $\sin b = \frac{\text{opp.}}{\text{hyp.}} = \frac{3}{5}$ and $\cos b = \frac{\text{adj.}}{\text{hyp.}} = \frac{4}{5}$.

c i

$$\begin{aligned}\sin(a-b) &= \sin a\cos b - \cos a\sin b \\ &= \frac{3}{\sqrt{13}} \times \frac{4}{5} - \frac{2}{\sqrt{13}} \times \frac{3}{5} \\ &= \frac{12}{5\sqrt{13}} - \frac{6}{5\sqrt{13}} \\ &= \frac{6}{5\sqrt{13}}\end{aligned}$$

> Using: $\sin(A-B) = \sin A\cos B - \cos A\sin B$

ii

$$\begin{aligned}\sin(b-a) &= -\sin(-(b-a)) \\ &= -\sin(a-b) \\ &= -\frac{6}{5\sqrt{13}}.\end{aligned}$$

> Remember: $\sin x = -\sin(-x)$ (think about the graph)

> You could also use the addition formula again but this is more work.

2010 Paper 2

1

See **Vectors** – (a) and (b) §2, §5 and §6, (c) §12

a From the diagram...

- R has coordinates $(0, 2, 0)$ so M is the point $(0, 1, 0)$.
- N lies $\frac{2}{3}$ of the way along $\overrightarrow{QU}$ so $N(4, 2, 2)$.

b Again from the diagram V is the point $(0, 2, 3)$.

$$\overrightarrow{VM} = \underline{m} - \underline{v} = \begin{pmatrix} 0 \\ 1 \\ 0 \end{pmatrix} - \begin{pmatrix} 0 \\ 2 \\ 3 \end{pmatrix} = \begin{pmatrix} 0 \\ -1 \\ -3 \end{pmatrix}$$

$$\overrightarrow{VN} = \underline{n} - \underline{v} = \begin{pmatrix} 4 \\ 2 \\ 2 \end{pmatrix} - \begin{pmatrix} 0 \\ 2 \\ 3 \end{pmatrix} = \begin{pmatrix} 4 \\ 0 \\ -1 \end{pmatrix}$$

c $M\hat{V}N$ is the angle between $\overrightarrow{VM}$ and $\overrightarrow{VN}$.

$$|\overrightarrow{VM}| = \sqrt{0^2 + (-1)^2 + (-3)^2} = \sqrt{10}$$

$$|\overrightarrow{VN}| = \sqrt{4^2 + 0^2 + (-1)^2} = \sqrt{17}$$

Method 1

$$\cos M\hat{V}N = \frac{\overrightarrow{VM} . \overrightarrow{VN}}{|\overrightarrow{VM}||\overrightarrow{VN}|}$$

Using: $\underline{a} . \underline{b} = |\underline{a}||\underline{b}|\cos\theta$

$$= \frac{0 \times 4 + (-1) \times 0 + (-3) \times (-1)}{\sqrt{10}\sqrt{17}}$$

$$= \frac{3}{\sqrt{10}\sqrt{17}}$$

$$M\hat{V}N = \cos^{-1}\left(\frac{3}{\sqrt{10}\sqrt{17}}\right)$$

$$= 76 \cdot 70 \text{ (to 2 d.p.)}$$

OR $1 \cdot 339$ rads (to 3 d.p.)

cont...

2010

Method 2 $|\vec{MN}| = \left|\begin{pmatrix}4\\1\\2\end{pmatrix}\right| = \sqrt{16+1+4} = \sqrt{21}$.

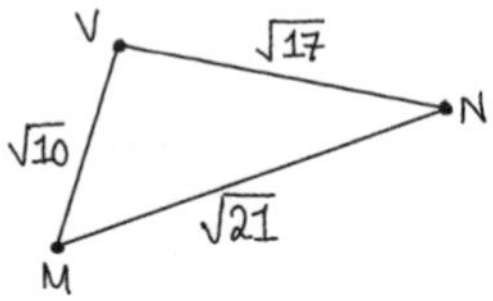

$$\cos M\hat{V}N = \frac{10+17-21}{2\sqrt{10}\sqrt{17}} = \frac{3}{\sqrt{10}\sqrt{17}}$$

Remember the cosine rule: $\cos A = \dfrac{b^2+c^2-a^2}{2bc}$

So $M\hat{V}N = 76 \cdot 70^\circ$ (to 2 d.p.) OR $1 \cdot 339$ rads (to 3 d.p.)

2

See **Wave Functions** – *(a)* §2, *(b)* §4

a

$$12\cos x^\circ - 5\sin x^\circ = k\cos(x^\circ + a^\circ)$$
$$= k\cos x^\circ \cos a^\circ - k\sin a^\circ \sin x^\circ$$
$$= (k\cos a^\circ)\cos x^\circ - (k\sin a^\circ)\sin x^\circ$$

Comparing coefficients: $k\cos a^\circ = 12$, $k\sin a^\circ = 5$

So $k = \sqrt{12^2+5^2} = \sqrt{169} = 13$ and $\tan a^\circ = \dfrac{k\sin a^\circ}{k\cos a^\circ} = \dfrac{5}{12}$.

$$a = \tan^{-1}\left(\frac{5}{12}\right) = 22 \cdot 62 \text{ (to 2 d.p.)}$$

So $12\cos x^\circ - 5\sin x^\circ = 13\cos(x^\circ + 22 \cdot 62^\circ)$.

b i The maximum value is 13 and the minimum value is -13.

ii The "$+22 \cdot 62^\circ$" shifts the graph of $y = 13\cos x^\circ$ to the left.

So the maximum occurs at

$x = 360 - 22 \cdot 62 = 337 \cdot 38$

and the minimum occurs at

$x = 180 - 22 \cdot 62 = 157 \cdot 38$

and only at these values in the interval $0 \leq x < 360$.

Sketch:

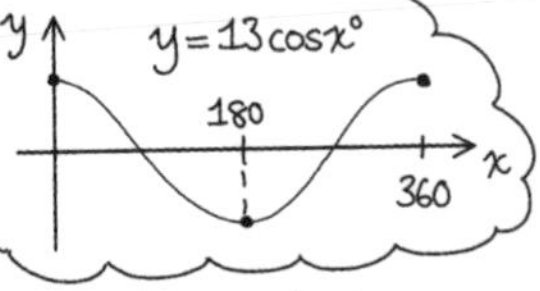

3

(a) See **Circles** *§5*
(b) See **Circles** *§3 and §1, and* **Vectors** *§10*

a i Put $y = 3 - x$ in the equation of the circle:

$$x^2 + (3-x)^2 + 14x + 4(3-x) - 19 = 0$$
$$x^2 + 9 - 6x + x^2 + 14x + 12 - 4x - 19 = 0$$
$$2x^2 + 4x + 2 = 0$$
$$2(x^2 + 2x + 1) = 0$$
$$(x+1)^2 = 0$$
$$x = -1.$$

You could also use the discriminant to show there is just one solution

Since there is only one solution, the line is a tangent.

ii When $x = -1$, $y = 3 - (-1) = 4$. So P is the point $(-1, 4)$.

b The larger circle has centre $D(-7, -2)$ and radius $\sqrt{(-7)^2 + (-2)^2 + 19}$
$= \sqrt{72}$
$= 6\sqrt{2}$ units.

The circle $x^2 + y^2 + 2gx + 2fy + c = 0$ has centre $(-g, -f)$ and radius $\sqrt{g^2 + f^2 - c}$

So the radius of the smaller circle is $\frac{1}{3} \times 6\sqrt{2} = 2\sqrt{2}$ units.

To find C...

$$\overrightarrow{DP} = 3\overrightarrow{PC}$$
$$\underline{p} - \underline{d} = 3(\underline{c} - \underline{p})$$
$$3\underline{c} = 4\underline{p} - \underline{d}$$
$$= \begin{pmatrix} -4 \\ 16 \end{pmatrix} - \begin{pmatrix} -7 \\ -2 \end{pmatrix}$$
$$= \begin{pmatrix} 3 \\ 18 \end{pmatrix}$$
$$\underline{c} = \begin{pmatrix} 1 \\ 6 \end{pmatrix}$$

So C is the point $(1, 6)$.

So the smaller circle has equation $(x-1)^2 + (y-6)^2 = (2\sqrt{2})^2 = 8$.

4

See **Trigonometry** §5

$$2\cos 2x - 5\cos x - 4 = 0$$
$$2(2\cos^2 x - 1) - 5\cos x - 4 = 0$$
$$4\cos^2 x - 5\cos x - 6 = 0$$
$$(4\cos x + 3)(\cos x - 2) = 0$$

Using: $\cos 2A = 2\cos^2 A - 1$

$\cos x = -\frac{3}{4}$

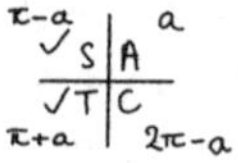

or $\cos x = 2$ ← no solutions

$$a = \cos^{-1}\left(\tfrac{3}{4}\right) = 0.723 \text{ (to 3 d.p.)}$$

$x = \pi - 0.723$ or $\pi + 0.723$

$= 2.419$ or 3.865

5

(*a*) See **Straight Lines** §1
(*b*) See **Differentiation** §12

a i When $x = 0$ on the lower curve, $y = \frac{2}{5}(10 - 0) = 4$. So $T(0,4)$.

Since $TP = x$, the x-coordinate of P is x.

So Q has y-coordinate $y = 10 - x^2$.

P and Q have x-coordinate 4, so PQ is the difference in y-coordinates.

Hence $PQ = 10 - x^2 - 4 = 6 - x^2$ units.

ii The shaded area is $A(x) = 2 \times x \times (6 - x^2) = 12x - 2x^3$.

b Stationary points exist where $A'(x) = 0$.

$$A'(x) = 12 - 6x^2 = 0$$
$$x^2 = 2$$
$$x = \pm\sqrt{2}.$$

Since x is a length (ie not negative) $x = \sqrt{2}$.

When $x = \sqrt{2}$, $A(\sqrt{2}) = 12\sqrt{2} - 2\sqrt{2}^3 = 8\sqrt{2}$.

cont...

Justify nature...

Method 1 Nature table:

x	$\sqrt{2}^-$	$\sqrt{2}$	$\sqrt{2}^+$
$A'(x)$	+	0	−
Sketch	/	—	\

Method 2 Second derivative test: $A''(x) = -12x$.

When $x = \sqrt{2}$, $A''(\sqrt{2}) = -12\sqrt{2} < 0$.

So the maximum area is $8\sqrt{2}$ square units which occurs when $x = \sqrt{2}$.

6

(a) See ***Further Calculus*** *§3 and §4, and* ***Differentiation*** *§5*
(c) See ***Integration*** *§5, §6 and §7*

a Using the chain rule...

$$\frac{dy}{dx} = \frac{1}{2}(2x-9)^{-1/2} \times \frac{d}{dx}(2x)$$

Remember: $\frac{dy}{dx} = m_{\text{tangent}}$

$$= \frac{1}{2} \cdot \frac{1}{\sqrt{2x-9}} \times 2$$

$$= \frac{1}{\sqrt{2x-9}}$$

When $x = 9$, $\frac{dy}{dx} = \frac{1}{\sqrt{9}} = \frac{1}{3}$.

and $y = (18-9)^{1/2} = \sqrt{9} = 3$.

So the equation of the tangent is

$$y - 3 = \frac{1}{3}(x-9)$$

$$3y - 9 = x - 9$$

$$y = \frac{1}{3}x.$$

cont...

2010

b Put $y = 0$ in the equation of the curve...

$$\sqrt{2x-9} = 0$$
$$2x - 9 = 0$$
$$x = \frac{9}{2}.$$

So A is the point $\left(\frac{9}{2}, 0\right)$.

c <u>Method 1</u>

Calculate the area of the large triangle between $x = 0$ and $x = 9$, then subtract the area under the curve between A and $x = 9$.

The area of the triangle is $\frac{1}{2} \times \text{base} \times \text{height} = \frac{1}{2} \times 9 \times 3 = \frac{27}{2}$.

The area under the curve is

$$\int_{9/2}^{9} (2x-9)^{1/2}\,dx = \left[\frac{(2x-9)^{3/2}}{\frac{3}{2} \times 2}\right]_{9/2}^{9}$$
$$= \left[\frac{1}{3}(2x-9)^{3/2}\right]_{9/2}^{9}$$
$$= \left(\frac{1}{3} \times 3^3 - 0\right)$$
$$= 9$$

Remember:
$$\int (ax+b)^n\,dx = \frac{(ax+b)^{n+1}}{a(n+1)} + c$$

So the shaded area is $\frac{27}{2} - 9 = \frac{9}{2}$ (or $4\frac{1}{2}$) square units.

cont...

2010

Method 2 Rearrange for x and integrate with respect to y.

Curve: $y=\sqrt{2x-9}$
$y^2=2x-9$
$x=\frac{1}{2}(y^2+9)$

Line: $y=\frac{1}{3}x$
$x=3y$.

The shaded area lies between the line and curve and $y=0$ and $y=3$, so is given by

$$\int_0^3 (\text{upper}-\text{lower})\,dy = \int_0^3\left(\frac{1}{2}(y^2+9)-3y\right)dy$$
$$=\int_0^3\left(\frac{1}{2}y^2-3y+\frac{9}{2}\right)dy$$
$$=\left[\frac{1}{6}y^3-\frac{3}{2}y^2+\frac{9}{2}y\right]_0^3$$
$$=\frac{1}{6}\times3^3-\frac{3}{2}\times3^2+\frac{9}{2}\times3$$
$$=\frac{9}{2}\quad\left(=4\frac{1}{2}\right)$$

Hence the shaded area is $\frac{9}{2}$ $\left(\text{or } 4\frac{1}{2}\right)$ square units.

7

See **Exponentials and Logarithms** §3

a

$\log_4 x = P$
$\Leftrightarrow\quad 4^P = x$
$\log_{16} 4^P = \log_{16} x$
$P.\log_{16} 4 = \log_{16} x$
$\log_{16} x = \frac{1}{2}P.\quad$ since $\log_{16} 4 = \frac{1}{2}$

Remember
$\log_a b$ is the power of a that gives b.

b Similarly, $\log_3 x = 2\log_9 x$. So the equation becomes

$2\log_9 x + \log_9 x = 12$
$\log_9 x = 4$
$x = 9^4$

Remember:
$\log_a x = b \Leftrightarrow x = a^b$.

2010

2011 Paper 1

1

See **Vectors** §5 and §6

$$2\underset{\sim}{p} - \underset{\sim}{q} - \tfrac{1}{2}\underset{\sim}{r} = 2\begin{pmatrix}2\\5\\-7\end{pmatrix} - \begin{pmatrix}1\\0\\-1\end{pmatrix} - \frac{1}{2}\begin{pmatrix}-4\\2\\0\end{pmatrix}$$

$$= \begin{pmatrix}4\\10\\-14\end{pmatrix} - \begin{pmatrix}1\\0\\-1\end{pmatrix} - \begin{pmatrix}-2\\1\\0\end{pmatrix}$$

$$= \begin{pmatrix}5\\9\\-13\end{pmatrix}.$$

C

2

See **Straight Lines** §3 and §6

Any line parallel to l has the same gradient.

To extract the gradient, rearrange to give $y = mx + c$...

$$3y + 2x = 6$$

$$3y = -2x + 6$$

$$y = -\frac{2}{3}x + 2.$$

So l has gradient $-\frac{2}{3}$.

B

3

See **Functions and Graphs** §10

The graph of $y = f(x+2) - 1$ is $y = f(x)$ shifted

- 2 units to the left and
- 1 unit down.

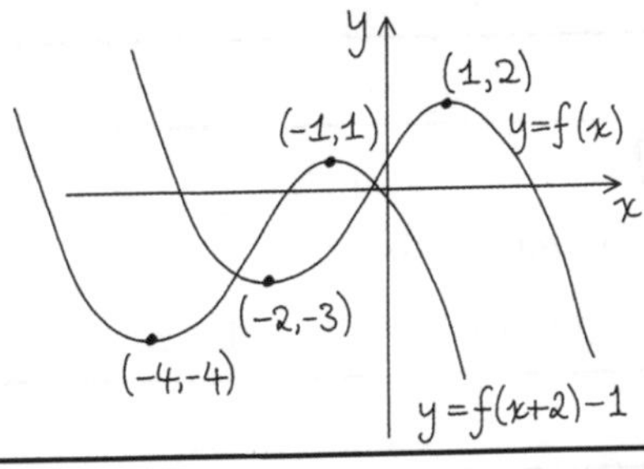

D

4

See **Differentiation** §5

$$\frac{dy}{dx} = 3x^2 - 2$$

Remember: the derivative gives the gradient of the tangent.

When $x = 2$, the gradient of the tangent is $3 \times 2^2 - 2 = 10$.

D

5

See **Polynomials and Quadratics** §3

Method 1 Compensating...

$x^2 - 8x + 7 = (x-4)^2 - 16 + 7 = (x-4)^2 - 9$. So $q = -9$

(This gives the correct x^2 and x terms, and an extra 16)

(Take off this extra 16)

Method 2 Comparing coefficients...

$$x^2 - 8x + 7 = (x-p)^2 + q$$
$$= x^2 - 2px + p^2 + q.$$

So $-2p = -8$ and $p^2 + q = 7$

$p = 4$ $q = 7 - 16$

$= -9$

A

6

See **Circles** §6

The tangent is perpendicular to CP so $m_{CP} \times m_{tgt} = -1$; hence $m_{tgt} = \frac{1}{2}$.

So the equation is $y - (-3) = \frac{1}{2}(x-2)$ using $P(2,-3)$.

$$y + 3 = \frac{1}{2}(x-2)$$

C

7

See **Polynomials and Quadratics** §9

The remainder is

$$f(1) = 1^3 - 1^2 + 1 + 3 = 4$$

(You could have used synthetic division)

D

8

See **Straight Lines** §3 and **Functions and Graphs** §8

$m = \tan\theta = \tan 30° = \frac{1}{\sqrt{3}}$.

(Exact values...)

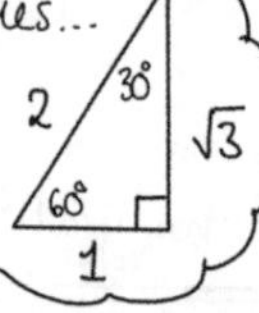

A

9

See **Polynomials and Quadratics** §2

Since $23>0$, the equation has real roots. So (1) is correct.

The roots could be rational or irrational, e.g.

- $\frac{1}{2}x^2+5x+1=0$ has solutions $x=-5\pm\sqrt{23}$.
- $\sqrt{23}\,x^2+\sqrt{23}\,x=0$ has solutions $x=0$, $x=-1$.

Hence statement (2) is not true in general.

B

10

See **Trigonometry** §1

$$2\cos x=\sqrt{3}$$

$$\cos x=\frac{\sqrt{3}}{2}$$

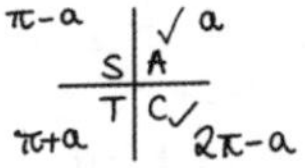

$$a=\cos^{-1}\left(\frac{\sqrt{3}}{2}\right)=\frac{\pi}{6}$$

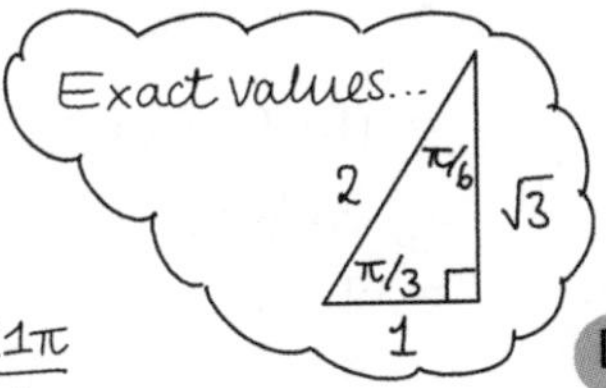

So $x=\frac{\pi}{6}$ or $2\pi-\frac{\pi}{6}=\frac{11\pi}{6}$

D

11

See **Integration** §1

$$\int\left(4x^{1/2}+x^{-3}\right)dx=\frac{4x^{3/2}}{3/2}+\frac{x^{-2}}{-2}+c=\frac{8}{3}x^{3/2}-\frac{1}{2}x^{-2}+c.$$

D

12

See **Trigonometry** §3

$\sin(p+q)=\sin p\cos q+\cos p\sin q$ ← (Using the formulae list)

From the diagram,

$$\sin p=\frac{\text{opp.}}{\text{hyp.}}=\frac{2}{\sqrt{5}},\quad \cos p=\frac{\text{adj.}}{\text{hyp.}}=\frac{1}{\sqrt{5}},$$

$$\sin q=\frac{2}{3}\quad\text{and}\quad\cos q=\frac{\sqrt{5}}{3}.$$

So $\sin(p+q)=\frac{2}{\sqrt{5}}\times\frac{\sqrt{5}}{3}+\frac{1}{\sqrt{5}}\times\frac{2}{3}=\frac{2}{3}+\frac{2}{3\sqrt{5}}.$

C

13

See **Further Calculus** §1

$f(x) = 4\sin 3x$

$f'(x) = 4 \times 3\cos 3x$
$\quad = 12\cos 3x$

Using: $\frac{d}{dx}(\sin ax) = a\cos ax$.

So $f'(0) = 12\cos(0) = 12$.

C

14

See **Vectors** §11

Since the triangle is equilateral, the angle θ between $\underset{\sim}{p}$ and $\underset{\sim}{q}$ is $60°$.

$\underset{\sim}{p} \cdot \underset{\sim}{q} = |\underset{\sim}{p}||\underset{\sim}{q}|\cos\theta$
$\quad = 3 \times 3 \times \cos 60°$
$\quad = 9 \times \frac{1}{2}$
$\quad = \frac{9}{2}$.

Exact values...

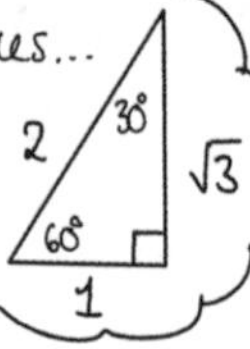

B

15

See **Vectors** §10

$\overrightarrow{ST} = \underset{\sim}{t} - \underset{\sim}{s} = \begin{pmatrix}-16\\-4\\16\end{pmatrix} - \begin{pmatrix}-4\\5\\1\end{pmatrix} = \begin{pmatrix}-12\\-9\\15\end{pmatrix} = -3\begin{pmatrix}4\\3\\-5\end{pmatrix}$

$\overrightarrow{TU} = \underset{\sim}{u} - \underset{\sim}{t} = \begin{pmatrix}-24\\-10\\26\end{pmatrix} - \begin{pmatrix}-16\\-4\\16\end{pmatrix} = \begin{pmatrix}-8\\-6\\10\end{pmatrix} = -2\begin{pmatrix}4\\3\\-5\end{pmatrix} = \frac{2}{3}\overrightarrow{ST}$

So $\frac{ST}{TU} = \frac{3}{2}$, i.e. T divides SU in the ratio 3:2.

B

16

See **Integration** §1 and §2

$\int \frac{1}{3x^4}\,dx = \frac{1}{3}\int x^{-4}\,dx = \frac{1}{3} \times \frac{x^{-3}}{-3} + c = -\frac{1}{9x^3} + c$.

A

2011

17

See **Polynomials and Quadratics** §12

The cubic crosses the x-axis at $x = -1$, $x = 0$ and $x = 2$; so its equation is

$$y = k(x-(-1))x(x-2) = kx(x+1)(x-2)$$

for some constant k.

When $x = 1$, $y = 2$ so $2 = k \times 1 \times 2 \times (-1)$ i.e. $k = -1$.

A

18

See **Polynomials and Quadratics** §6

The graph is above the x-axis when

$$(x-3)(x+5) > 0.$$

From the sketch, $x < -5$ or $x > 3$.

Sketch:

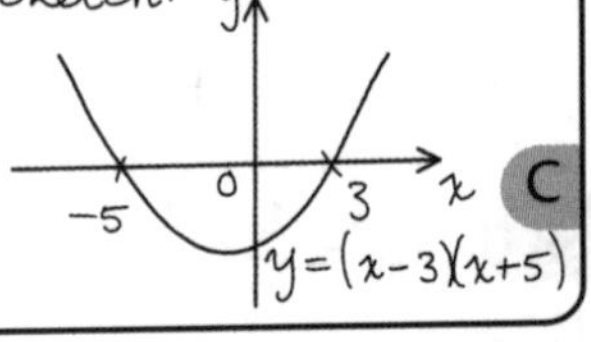

C

19

See **Exponentials and Logarithms** §2 and **Functions and Graphs** §5

When $x = 1$, $\log_3 y = 1$ i.e. $y = 3^1 = 3$

When $x = 0$, $\log_3 y = 0$ i.e. $y = 3^0 = 1$.

Remember: $x = \log_a y \Leftrightarrow y = a^x$.

So the curve passes through $(1,3)$ and $(0,1)$

C

20

See **Functions and Graphs** §2, §3 and §9

$g(x) = \sin^2\sqrt{x-2}$.

Since we are taking the square root of $x-2$, we need

$x - 2 \geq 0$ i.e. $x \geq 2$.

Since $\sqrt{x-2}$ can have any value ≥ 0, $-1 \leq \sin\sqrt{x-2} \leq 1$.

Hence $0 \leq g(x) \leq 1$.

D

2011

21

See **Straight Lines** – *(a) §6, (b) §10, (c) §9 and §6*

a

$$m_{BD} = \frac{-3-12}{2-7} = \frac{-15}{-5} = 3.$$

So the equation of BD is $y-(-3) = 3(x-2)$ using $D(2,-3)$.

$$y+3 = 3x-6$$
$$3x-y-9=0.$$

b Solve the equations of BD and AC simultaneously...

$$3x - y = 9 \quad \text{—— ①}$$
$$x + 3y = 23 \quad \text{—— ②}$$

$3\times① + ②$: $\quad 10x = 50$

$$x = 5$$

Put $x=5$ into ①: $y = 3\times5-9 = 6$. So E is the point $(5,6)$.

c i

$$m_{AB} = \frac{12-8}{7+1} = \frac{4}{8} = \frac{1}{2}.$$ So $m_{\perp} = -2$ since $m_{AB}\times m_{\perp} = -1$.

$$\text{midpoint}_{AB} = \left(\frac{-1+7}{2}, \frac{8+12}{2}\right) = (3,10).$$

Then the equation of the perpendicular bisector is

$$y-10 = -2(x-3)$$
$$y-10 = -2x+6$$
$$y+2x-16=0. \quad \text{———— } (*)$$

ii Put $x=5$ and $y=6$ in the left-hand side of $(*)$ and check we get the right-hand side...

$$6+2\times5-16=0.$$

So the line passes through E.

2011

22

(a) See **Differentiation** *§9*
(b) See **Differentiation** *§7 and §8*
(c) See **Functions and Graphs** *§10*

a i The curve cuts the x-axis when $y=0$ i.e.

$$(x-2)(x^2+1)=0$$

$$x=2 \quad \text{or} \quad x^2=-1 \leftarrow \text{no real solutions}$$

So the curve cuts the x-axis at $(2,0)$.

ii The curve cuts the y-axis when $x=0$ i.e.

$$y=(0-2)(0^2+1)=-2.$$

So the curve cuts the y-axis at $(0,-2)$.

b Stationary points exist where $f'(x)=0$.

$$f(x)=(x-2)(x^2+1)=x^3-2x^2+x-2$$

$$f'(x)=3x^2-4x+1=0$$

$$(3x-1)(x-1)=0.$$

$$x=\frac{1}{3} \text{ and } x=1.$$

When $x=\frac{1}{3}$, $y=\left(\frac{1}{3}-2\right)\left(\left(\frac{1}{3}\right)^2+1\right)=-\frac{5}{3}\times\frac{10}{9}=-\frac{50}{27}$.

When $x=1$, $y=(1-2)(1^2+1)=-2$.

So the stationary points are $\left(\frac{1}{3},-\frac{50}{27}\right)$ and $(1,-2)$.

Justify nature...

<u>**Method 1**</u> Nature table:

x	$\frac{1}{3}^-$	$\frac{1}{3}$	$\frac{1}{3}^+$	1^-	1	1^+
$f'(x)$	+	0	−	+	0	−
Sketch	/	—	\	\	—	/

<u>**Method 2**</u> Second derivative test: $f''(x)=6x-4$

When $x=\frac{1}{3}$, $f''\left(\frac{1}{3}\right)=6\times\frac{1}{3}-4=-2<0$.

When $x=1$, $f''(1)=6\times1-4=2>0$

So $\left(\frac{1}{3},-\frac{50}{27}\right)$ is a maximum turning point

$(1,-2)$ is a minimum turning point.

cont...

2011

c i

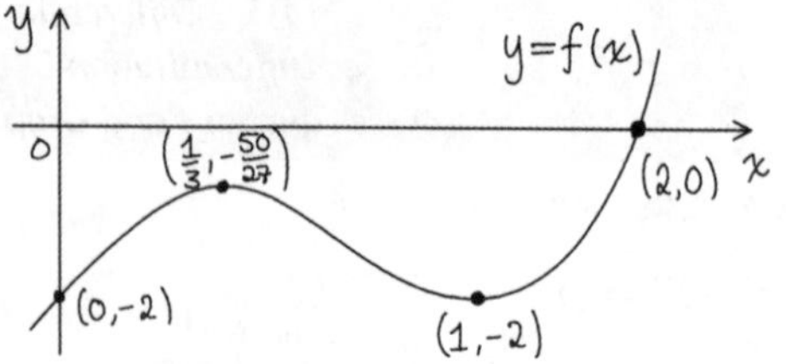

ii For the graph of $y=-f(x)$, reflect in the x-axis.

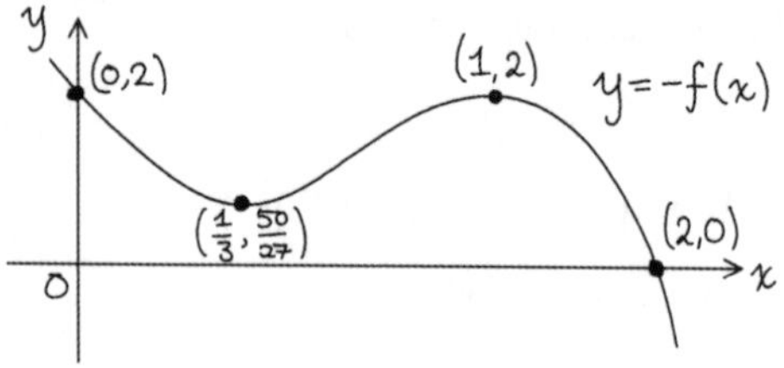

23

See **Trigonometry** §4 and §5

a

$$\cos 2x° - 3\cos x° + 2 = 0$$
$$2\cos^2 x° - 1 - 3\cos x° + 2 = 0$$
$$2\cos^2 x° - 3\cos x° + 1 = 0$$
$$(2\cos x° - 1)(\cos x° - 1) = 0.$$

Using: $\cos 2A = 2\cos^2 A - 1$

$2\cos x° - 1 = 0$

$\cos x° = \frac{1}{2}$

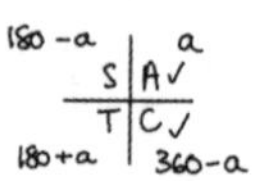

$a = \cos^{-1}\left(\frac{1}{2}\right)$

$= 60$

or

$\cos x° - 1 = 0$

$\cos x° = 1$

$x = 0$

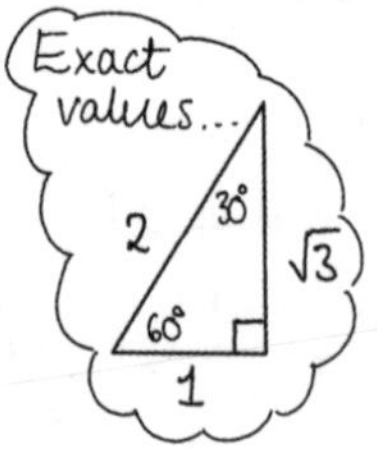

$x = 60$ or $360 - 60$

So $x = 0, 60$ or 300

b Let $u = 2x$, then the equation becomes

$$\cos 2u° - 3\cos u° + 2 = 0.$$

Since $0 \leq x < 360$, $0 \leq u < 720$.

From part (a), $u = 0, 60, 300, 360, 420, 660,$ ~~720~~ ← too big

So $x = 0, 30, 150, 180, 210, 330.$

2011 Paper 2

1

See **Vectors** – *(a) §2 and §5, (b) §7, and (c) §12*

a B(4,4,0) since OABC is a square with side length 4.

b

$$\overrightarrow{DB} = \underline{b} - \underline{d} = \begin{pmatrix}4\\4\\0\end{pmatrix} - \begin{pmatrix}2\\2\\6\end{pmatrix} = \begin{pmatrix}2\\2\\-6\end{pmatrix}$$

M lies half-way along OA, so M is (2,0,0).

$$\overrightarrow{DM} = \underline{m} - \underline{d} = \begin{pmatrix}2\\0\\0\end{pmatrix} - \begin{pmatrix}2\\2\\6\end{pmatrix} = \begin{pmatrix}0\\-2\\-6\end{pmatrix}$$

c $B\hat{D}M$ is the angle between $\overrightarrow{DB}$ and $\overrightarrow{DM}$

$$|\overrightarrow{DB}| = \sqrt{2^2 + 2^2 + (-6)^2} = \sqrt{44} = 2\sqrt{11}$$

$$|\overrightarrow{DM}| = \sqrt{0^2 + (-2)^2 + (-6)^2} = \sqrt{40} = 2\sqrt{10}$$

Method 1

$$\cos B\hat{D}M = \frac{\overrightarrow{DB} \cdot \overrightarrow{DM}}{|\overrightarrow{DB}||\overrightarrow{DM}|}$$

Using: $\underline{a} \cdot \underline{b} = |\underline{a}||\underline{b}|\cos\theta$

$$= \frac{2\times0 + 2\times(-2) + (-6)\times(-6)}{4\sqrt{10}\sqrt{11}}$$

$$= \frac{8}{\sqrt{10}\sqrt{11}}$$

$$B\hat{D}M = \cos^{-1}\left(\frac{8}{\sqrt{10}\sqrt{11}}\right)$$

$= 40.29°$ (to 2 d.p.)

OR 0.703 rads (to 3 d.p.)

2011

cont...

Method 2 $|\overrightarrow{MB}| = \left|\begin{pmatrix}2\\4\\0\end{pmatrix}\right| = \sqrt{4+16} = \sqrt{20} = 2\sqrt{5}$

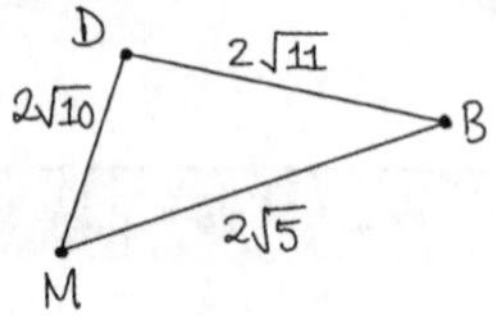

$$\cos B\hat{D}M = \frac{44+40-20}{8\sqrt{10}\sqrt{11}} = \frac{8}{\sqrt{10}\sqrt{11}}$$

Remember the cosine rule: $\cos A = \dfrac{b^2+c^2-a^2}{2bc}$

So $B\hat{D}M = 40{\cdot}29°$ (to 2 d.p.) OR $0{\cdot}703$ rads (to 3 d.p.)

2

(a) and (b) See **Functions and Graphs** §3
(c) and (d) See **Polynomials and Quadratics** §9

a $g(f(x)) = g(x^3-1) = 3(x^3-1)+1 = 3x^3-2$

b $g(f(x)) + xh(x) = 3x^3 - 2 + x(4x-5)$
$= 3x^3 - 2 + 4x^2 - 5x$
$= 3x^3 + 4x^2 - 5x - 2.$

c i $x-1$ is a factor $\Leftrightarrow$ the expression is zero when $x=1$.

Method 1 When $x=1$, $3(1)^3 + 4(1)^2 - 5(1) - 2 = 0$

Method 2 Using synthetic division...

1	3	4	−5	−2
		3	7	2
	3	7	2	0

Since the expression is zero, $x-1$ is a factor.

ii $3x^3+4x^2-5x-2 = (x-1)(3x^2+7x-2)$ ← By inspection or from the table.
$= (x-1)(3x+1)(x+2)$

d $g(f(x)) + xh(x) = 0$
$(x-1)(3x+1)(x+2) = 0$
$x = 1$ or $x = -\frac{1}{3}$ or $x = -2$.

2011

3

See **Sequences** – (a) §2, (b) §5, (c) §4

a

$u_0 = -16$

$u_1 = -\frac{1}{2}u_0 = -\frac{1}{2}\times(-16) = 8$

$u_2 = -\frac{1}{2}\times u_1 = -\frac{1}{2}\times 8 = -4$

b We know that $v_2 = 5$ and $v_3 = 7$, so $5 = 4p + q$ and $7 = 5p + q$.

Solving simultaneously...

$5 = 4p + q$ —— ①
$7 = 5p + q$ —— ②

②−①: $p = 2$.

When $p = 2$, $q = 5 - 4\times 2 = -3$.

c i Since $-1 < -\frac{1}{2} < 1$, the sequence in (a) has a limit.

Method 1 $l = \frac{b}{1-a}$ with $a = -\frac{1}{2}$ and $b = 0$.

So $l = 0$.

Method 2 As $n \to \infty$, $u_{n+1} = u_n = l$

So $l = -\frac{1}{2}l$

$\frac{3}{2}l = 0$

$l = 0$

ii The sequence from (b) does not have a limit since $p = 2 > 1$.

2011

4

See **Integration** §6

The shaded area between $x=-2$ and $x=0$ is given by

$$\int_{-2}^{0}(\text{upper}-\text{lower})\,dx = \int_{-2}^{0}\left(x^3-x^2-4x+4-(2x+4)\right)dx$$
$$= \int_{-2}^{0}\left(x^3-x^2-6x\right)dx$$
$$= \left[\tfrac{1}{4}x^4-\tfrac{1}{3}x^3-3x^2\right]_{-2}^{0}$$
$$= 0-\left(\tfrac{1}{4}(-2)^4-\tfrac{1}{3}(-2)^3-3(-2)^2\right)$$
$$= -\frac{16}{4}-\frac{8}{3}+12$$
$$= 8-\frac{8}{3}$$
$$= \frac{16}{3}$$

Remember:
$$\int(ax+b)^n\,dx = \frac{(ax+b)^{n+1}}{a(n+1)}+c$$

The shaded area between $x=0$ and $x=3$ is given by

$$\int_{0}^{3}(\text{upper}-\text{lower})\,dx = \int_{0}^{3}\left(2x+4-(x^3-x^2-4x+4)\right)dx$$
$$= \int_{0}^{3}\left(-x^3+x^2+6x\right)dx$$
$$= \left[-\tfrac{1}{4}x^4+\tfrac{1}{3}x^3+3x^2\right]_{0}^{3}$$
$$= -\tfrac{1}{4}\times 3^4+\tfrac{1}{3}\times 3^3+3\times 3^2-0$$
$$= -\frac{81}{4}+9+27$$
$$= \frac{63}{4}$$

So the shaded area is $\frac{16}{3}+\frac{63}{4}=\frac{253}{12}$ (or $21\frac{1}{12}$) square units.

5

See **Exponentials and Logarithms** §6

We are told $y = kx^n$. Taking $\log_2$ gives

$$\begin{aligned} \log_2 y &= \log_2 (kx^n) \\ &= \log_2 k + \log_2 x^n \\ &= \log_2 k + n\log_2 x \\ &= n\log_2 x + \log_2 k. \end{aligned}$$

The line has gradient $\frac{7-5}{4-0} = \frac{1}{2}$, so $n = \frac{1}{2}$.

The line passes through $(0,5)$, so $\log_2 k = 5$ i.e. $k = 2^5 = 32$.

6

(a) See **Wave Functions** §1 and §2
(b) See **Further Calculus** §2 and **Trigonometry** §5

a

$$\begin{aligned} 3\sin x - 5\cos x &= R\sin(x+a) \\ &= R\sin x\cos a + R\cos x\sin a \\ &= (R\cos a)\sin x + (R\sin a)\cos x \end{aligned}$$

Comparing coefficients: $R\cos a = 3$, $R\sin a = -5$

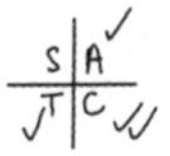

So $R = \sqrt{3^2 + (-5)^2} = \sqrt{34}$ and $\tan a = -\frac{5}{3}$

$$\begin{aligned} a &= 2\pi - \tan^{-1}\left(\tfrac{5}{3}\right) \\ &= 5{\cdot}253 \text{ (to 3 d.p.)} \end{aligned}$$

So $3\sin x - 5\cos x = \sqrt{34}\sin(x + 5{\cdot}253)$.

cont...

b

$$\int_0^t (3\cos x + 5\sin x)\,dx = \Big[3\sin x - 5\cos x\Big]_0^t$$
$$= 3\sin t - 5\cos t - (3\sin 0 - 5\cos 0)$$
$$= 3\sin t - 5\cos t + 5.$$

So the equation becomes

$$3\sin t - 5\cos t + 5 = 3$$
$$\sqrt{34}\,\sin(t + 5{\cdot}253) = -2$$
$$\sin(t + 5{\cdot}253) = -\frac{2}{\sqrt{34}}$$

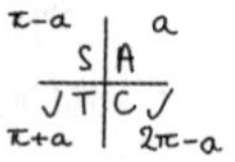

$$a = \sin^{-1}\left(\frac{2}{\sqrt{34}}\right)$$
$$= 0{\cdot}350 \text{ (to 3 d.p.)}$$

$$t + 5{\cdot}253 = \pi + 0{\cdot}350 \quad \text{or} \quad 2\pi - 0{\cdot}350$$
$$t = -1{\cdot}761 \quad \text{or} \quad 0{\cdot}680.$$

Since $0 \le t \le 2$, the solution is $t = 0{\cdot}68$ (to 2 d.p.).

7

See **Circles** §1, §3 and §7

Circle C_1 has centre $(-1, 1)$ and radius $r_1 = \sqrt{121} = 11$

Circle C_2 has centre $(2, -3)$ and radius $r_2 = \sqrt{2^2 + (-3)^2 + p} = \sqrt{13 - p}$

The distance between the centres is

$$d = \sqrt{(-3-1)^2 + (2+1)^2}$$
$$= \sqrt{25}$$
$$= 5.$$

Since the circles do not touch, $5 + r_2 < r_1$ i.e.

$$5 + \sqrt{13 - p} < 11$$
$$\sqrt{13 - p} < 6$$
$$13 - p < 36$$
$$p > -23.$$

The circle $(x-a)^2 + (y-b)^2 = r^2$ has centre (a, b) and radius r.

The circle $x^2 + y^2 + 2gx + 2fy + c = 0$ has centre $(-g, -f)$ and radius $\sqrt{g^2 + f^2 - c}$

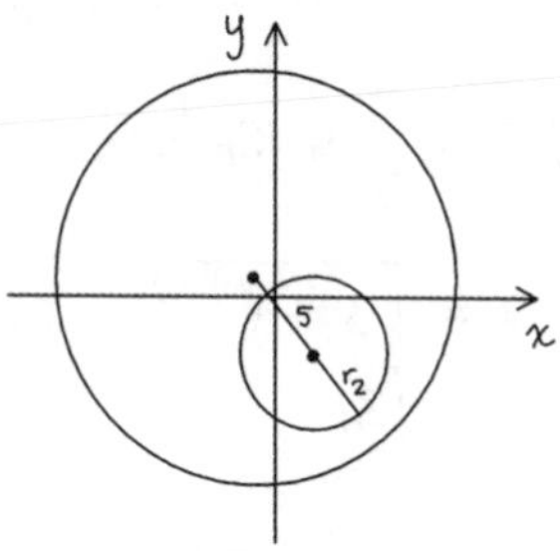

In addition we need $13 - p > 0$, since $r_2 = \sqrt{13 - p}$, ie $p < 13$.
Hence $-23 < p < 13$.

2012 Paper 1

1

See **Sequences** §2

$u_1 = 3u_0 + 4 = 3 \times 1 + 4 = 7$
$u_2 = 3u_1 + 4 = 3 \times 7 + 4 = 25$

C

2

See **Differentiation** §5

$\frac{dy}{dx} = 3x^2 - 6$

Remember: the derivative gives the gradient of the tangent.

When $x = -2$, the gradient of the tangent is $3 \times (-2)^2 - 6 = 6$.

D

3

See **Polynomials and Quadratics** §3

Method 1 Compensating...

$x^2 - 6x + 14 = (x-3)^2 - 9 + 14 = (x-3)^2 + 5.$

This gives the correct x^2 and x terms, and an extra 9

Take off this extra 9

Method 2 Comparing coefficients...

$x^2 - 6x + 14 = (x-p)^2 + q$
$= x^2 - 2px + p^2 + q$

So $-2p = -6$ and $p^2 + q = 14$
$p = 3$ $q = 14 - 9 = 5$

B

2012

4

See **Straight Lines** §3 and **Functions and Graphs** §8

$$m = \tan 150°$$
$$= -\tan 30°$$
$$= -\frac{1}{\sqrt{3}}$$

Exact values...

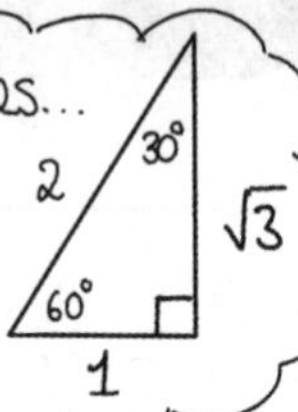

B

5

See **Trigonometry** §4

$$\cos 2a = 2\cos^2 a - 1$$
$$= 2 \times \left(\frac{4}{5}\right)^2 - 1$$
$$= \frac{32}{25} - 1$$
$$= \frac{7}{25}$$

Remember:
$\cos a = \frac{\text{adjacent}}{\text{hypotenuse}}$

A

6

See **Differentiation** §2

$$\frac{dy}{dx} = -2 \times 3x^{-3} + \frac{3}{2} \times 2x^{1/2} = -6x^{-3} + 3x^{1/2}$$

C

7

See **Vectors** §13

$\underline{u}$ and $\underline{v}$ are perpendicular $\Leftrightarrow$ $\underline{u}.\underline{v} = 0$.

$$\underline{u}.\underline{v} = 0$$
$$-3 + t - 2t = 0$$
$$t = -3.$$

A

8

See **Differentiation** §3 and §4

$$\frac{dV}{dr} = 3 \times \frac{4}{3}\pi r^2 = 4\pi r^2$$

When $r = 2$, $\frac{dV}{dr} = 4\pi \times 2^2 = 16\pi$.

Remember:
"rate of change"
means "derivative"

C

2012

9

See **Functions and Graphs** §10

The graph of $y = \cos x$ has been
- shifted down 1, so $b = -1$
- shifted right by $\pi/6$, so $a = -\frac{\pi}{6}$.

Therefore $y = \cos\left(x - \frac{\pi}{6}\right) - 1$.

A

10

See **Vectors** §5

$\overrightarrow{RP} = \overrightarrow{RS} + \overrightarrow{ST} + \overrightarrow{TP} = -\underline{g} - \underline{f} + \underline{h}$

B

11

See **Integration** §2

$$\begin{aligned} \int\left(\frac{1}{6x^2}\right)dx &= \int\left(\frac{1}{6}x^{-2}\right)dx \\ &= \frac{x^{-1}}{-6} + c \\ &= -\frac{1}{6}x^{-1} + c. \end{aligned}$$

D

12

See **Functions and Graphs** §9

The expression $2 - 3\sin\left(x - \frac{\pi}{3}\right)$ is maximal when $\sin\left(x - \frac{\pi}{3}\right)$ is minimal.

The minimum value of $\sin\left(x - \frac{\pi}{3}\right)$ is -1 when $x - \frac{\pi}{3} = \frac{3\pi}{2}$ ie $x = \frac{11\pi}{6}$.

And when $x = \frac{11\pi}{6}$, $2 - 3\sin\left(x - \frac{\pi}{3}\right) = 2 - 3 \times (-1) = 5$.

B

2012

13

See **Polynomials and Quadratics** §5

Let the equation of the parabola be $y = f(x)$.
Since $x = -1$ and $x = -2$ are zeros of the parabola, $(x+1)$ and $(x+2)$ are factors of $f(x)$. Thus

$$f(x) = k(x+1)(x+2)$$

for some constant k. Using the point $(0, 6)$,

$$f(0) = k \times 1 \times 2 = 6$$
$$\text{ie} \quad k = 3.$$

D

14

See **Further Calculus** §5

$$\int (2x-1)^{1/2}\,dx = \frac{(2x-1)^{3/2}}{3/2 \times 2} + c$$
$$= \frac{1}{3}(2x-1)^{3/2} + c.$$

Remember: $\int (ax+b)^n\,dx = \frac{(ax+b)^{n+1}}{a(n+1)} + c$

A

15

See **Vectors** §3

$$|\underline{u}| = k\left|\begin{pmatrix} 3 \\ -1 \\ 0 \end{pmatrix}\right| = k\sqrt{3^2 + (-1)^2} = \sqrt{10}\,k.$$

So $\sqrt{10}\,k = 1$ ie $k = \frac{1}{\sqrt{10}}$.

Remember: $\underline{u}$ a unit vector means $|\underline{u}| = 1$.

D

16

See **Further Calculus** §3

$$y = 3(\cos x)^4$$
$$\frac{dy}{dx} = 3 \times 4(\cos x)^3 \times (-\sin x)$$
$$= -12 \sin x \cos^3 x$$

Using
- the chain rule
- $\frac{d}{dx}(\cos x) = -\sin x$

C

2012

17

See **Vectors** §14

$$\underline{a}.(\underline{a}+\underline{b}) = \underline{a}.\underline{a} + \underline{a}.\underline{b}$$
$$7 = 3^2+4^2+\underline{a}.\underline{b}$$
$$\underline{a}.\underline{b} = 7-25$$
$$= -18.$$

D

18

See **Differentation** §11

The graph of $f(x)$ is strictly below the x-axis for $s<x<t$.
So statement (1) is correct.

Since $(0, p)$ is a stationary point, $f'(0)=0$.
Hence statement (2) is incorrect.

B

19

See **Polynomials and Quadratics** §6

$$-x^2-x+6 = -(x^2+x-6)$$
$$= -(x+3)(x-2)$$

Sketch:

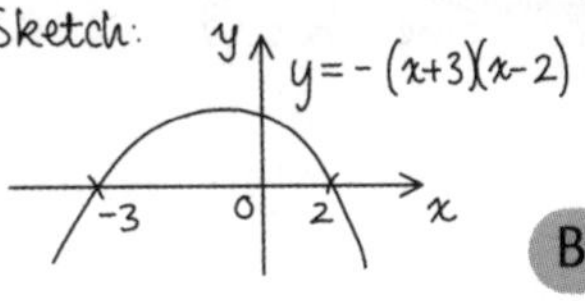

So $-(x+3)(x-2)<0$ when $x<-3$, $x>2$.

B

20

See **Exponentials and Logarithms** §3

$$\frac{\log_b 9a^2}{\log_b 3a} = \frac{\log_b (3a)^2}{\log_b 3a} = \frac{2\log_b 3a}{\log_b 3a} = 2.$$

Remember:
$\log_a (x)^n = n\log_a x.$

A

2012

21

(a) See **Polynomials and Quadratics** §9
(b) See **Integration** §5

a i Let $f(x) = x^3 - 5x^2 + 2x + 8$. Then $(x-4)$ is a factor $\Leftrightarrow$ $f(4) = 0$.

Method 1 $f(4) = 4^3 - 5 \times 4^2 + 2 \times 4 + 8 = 64 - 80 + 8 + 8 = 0$

Method 2 Using synthetic division...

4	1	-5	2	8
		4	-4	-8
	1	-1	-2	0

Since $f(4) = 0$, $(x-4)$ is a factor.

ii
$$\begin{aligned} x^3 - 5x^2 + 2x + 8 &= (x-4)(x^2 - x - 2) \\ &= (x-4)(x-2)(x+1) \end{aligned}$$

By inspection or from the table

iii
$$x^3 - 5x^2 + 2x + 8 = 0$$
$$(x-4)(x-2)(x+1) = 0$$
$x = 4$ or $x = 2$ or $x = -1$.

b Using part (a), the point Q has coordinates $(2,0)$.
The shaded area is given by

$$\begin{aligned} \int_0^2 (x^3 - 5x^2 + 2x + 8)\,dx &= \left[\tfrac{1}{4}x^4 - \tfrac{5}{3}x^3 + x^2 + 8x\right]_0^2 \\ &= \left(\tfrac{1}{4} \times 16 - \tfrac{5}{3} \times 8 + 4 + 16\right) - 0 \\ &= 4 - \tfrac{40}{3} + 4 + 16 \\ &= \tfrac{32}{3}. \end{aligned}$$

So the shaded area is $\frac{32}{3}$ $\left(\text{or } 10\frac{2}{3}\right)$ square units.

2012

22

See **Wave Functions** – (a) §2, (b) §5

a

$$\cos x - \sqrt{3}\sin x = k\cos(x+a)$$
$$= k\cos x\cos a - k\sin x\sin a$$
$$= (k\cos a)\cos x - (k\sin a)\sin x$$

Comparing coefficients: $k\cos a = 1$, $k\sin a = \sqrt{3}$

So $(k\sin a)^2 + (k\cos a)^2 = 3 + 1$ and $\tan a = \dfrac{k\sin a}{k\cos a} = \sqrt{3}$

$k^2 = 4$

$k = 2$ $\qquad a = \dfrac{\pi}{3}$

Therefore $\cos x - \sqrt{3}\sin x = 2\cos\left(x + \frac{\pi}{3}\right)$.

b When $x = 0$, $y = 2\cos\left(0 + \frac{\pi}{3}\right) = 2 \times \frac{1}{2} = 1$

So the graph crosses the y-axis at $(0, 1)$.

For the zeros solve, for $0 \leq x \leq 2\pi$,

$$2\cos\left(x + \frac{\pi}{3}\right) = 0$$
$$\cos\left(x + \frac{\pi}{3}\right) = 0$$
$$x + \frac{\pi}{3} = \frac{\pi}{2} \quad \text{or} \quad x + \frac{\pi}{3} = \frac{3\pi}{2}$$
$$x = \frac{\pi}{6} \qquad\qquad x = \frac{7\pi}{6}.$$

So the graph crosses the x-axis at $\left(\frac{\pi}{6}, 0\right)$ and $\left(\frac{7\pi}{6}, 0\right)$.

2012

23

See **Straight Lines** – *(a) §9, (b) §3 and §6, (c) §10, (d) §1*

a $\text{midpoint}_{PQ} = \left(\frac{3-1}{2}, \frac{-3+9}{2}\right) = (1,3)$

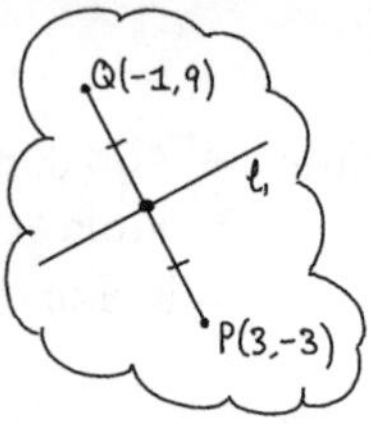

$m_{PQ} = \frac{9+3}{-1-3} = \frac{12}{-4} = -3.$

So $m_{\ell_1} = \frac{1}{3}$ since $m_{PQ} \times m_{\ell_1} = -1$.

Therefore the equation of ℓ_1 is

$$y - 3 = \frac{1}{3}(x-1)$$
$$3y - 9 = x - 1$$
$$x - 3y + 8 = 0.$$

b The gradient of ℓ_2 is -3 since it is parallel to PQ.

The equation of ℓ_2 is

$$y + 2 = -3(x-1)$$
$$y + 2 = -3x + 3$$
$$3x + y - 1 = 0.$$

c Solve the equations of ℓ_1 and ℓ_2 simultaneously ...

$$x - 3y = -8 \quad \text{①}$$
$$3x + y = 1 \quad \text{②}$$

①+3×②: $10x = -5$

$$x = -\frac{1}{2}$$

Put $x = -\frac{1}{2}$ into ②: $y = 1 - 3\times\left(-\frac{1}{2}\right) = 1 + \frac{3}{2} = \frac{5}{2}$.

So the point of intersection is $\left(-\frac{1}{2}, \frac{5}{2}\right)$

d The minimum distance is

$$d = \sqrt{\left(1+\frac{1}{2}\right)^2 + \left(3-\frac{5}{2}\right)^2}$$
$$= \sqrt{\left(\frac{3}{2}\right)^2 + \left(\frac{1}{2}\right)^2}$$
$$= \sqrt{\frac{10}{4}}$$
$$= \sqrt{\frac{5}{2}} \text{ units.}$$

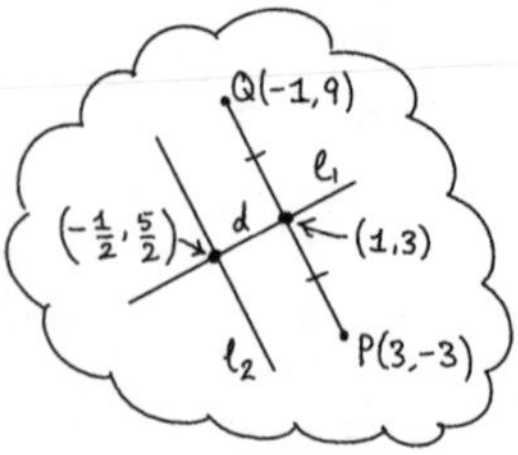

2012 Paper 2

1

(a) See **Functions and Graphs** §3
(b) See **Polynomials and Quadratics** §2

a i $f(g(x)) = f(x+4) = (x+4)^2 + 3.$

ii $g(f(x)) = g(x^2+3) = x^2+3+4 = x^2+7.$

b

$$f(g(x)) + g(f(x)) = 0$$
$$(x+4)^2 + 3 + x^2 + 7 = 0$$
$$x^2 + 8x + 16 + 3 + x^2 + 7 = 0$$
$$2x^2 + 8x + 26 = 0$$
$$x^2 + 4x + 13 = 0.$$

The discriminant is $4^2 - 4 \times 1 \times 13 = 16 - 52 < 0.$
So the equation has no real roots.

2

(a) See **Circles** §4
(b) See **Circles** §4 and **Vectors** §7

a The equation of the line is $y = 2x + 5.$

Put $y = 2x+5$ in the equation of the circle:

$$x^2 + (2x+5)^2 - 6x - 2(2x+5) - 30 = 0$$
$$x^2 + 4x^2 + 20x + 25 - 6x - 4x - 10 - 30 = 0$$
$$5x^2 + 10x - 15 = 0$$
$$x^2 + 2x - 3 = 0$$
$$(x+3)(x-1) = 0.$$
$$x = -3 \text{ or } x = 1.$$

When $x = -3$, $y = 2 \times (-3) + 5 = -1$. So P is the point $(-3, -1)$.
$x = 1$, $y = 2 \times 1 + 5 = 7$. So Q is the point $(1, 7)$.

cont...

b The circle from (a) has centre $(3, 1)$ and radius $\sqrt{3^2+1^2+30} = \sqrt{40}$ units.

The circle $x^2+y^2+2gx+2fy+c=0$ has centre $(-g,-f)$ and radius $\sqrt{g^2+f^2-c}$.

From the picture we see that

$$\begin{aligned} \underline{d} &= \underline{c} + \overrightarrow{CP} + \overrightarrow{CQ} \\ &= \underline{c} + \underline{p} - \underline{c} + \underline{q} - \underline{c} \\ &= \underline{p} + \underline{q} - \underline{c} \\ &= \begin{pmatrix} -3 \\ -1 \end{pmatrix} + \begin{pmatrix} 1 \\ 7 \end{pmatrix} - \begin{pmatrix} 3 \\ 1 \end{pmatrix} \\ &= \begin{pmatrix} -5 \\ 5 \end{pmatrix}. \end{aligned}$$

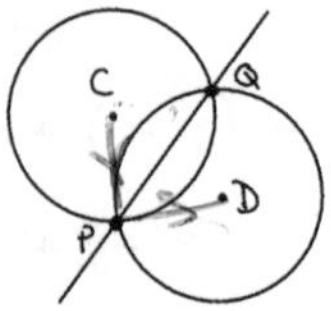

So D is the point $(-5,5)$.

So the equation of the second circle is $(x+5)^2+(y-5)^2 = 40$.

3

See **Differentiation** §10

The maximum and minimum occur at a turning point or at an endpoint of the interval $0 \leqslant x \leqslant 3$.

Stationary points exist where $f'(x)=0$.

$$\begin{aligned} f'(x) = 3x^2-4x-4 &= 0 \\ (3x+2)(x-2) &= 0 \\ x = -\tfrac{2}{3} \quad &\text{or} \quad x = 2. \end{aligned}$$

($x = -\tfrac{2}{3}$: Not in $0 \leqslant x \leqslant 3$)

Then $f(2) = 2^3 - 2\times 2^2 - 4\times 2 + 6 = -2.$ ← minimum

$f(0) = 6$ ← maximum.

$f(3) = 3^3 - 2\times 3^2 - 4\times 3 + 6 = 3.$

So the minimum value of f is -2 and the maximum value is 6.

4

(a) See **Differentiation** *§11*
(b) See **Functions and Graphs** *§10*

a

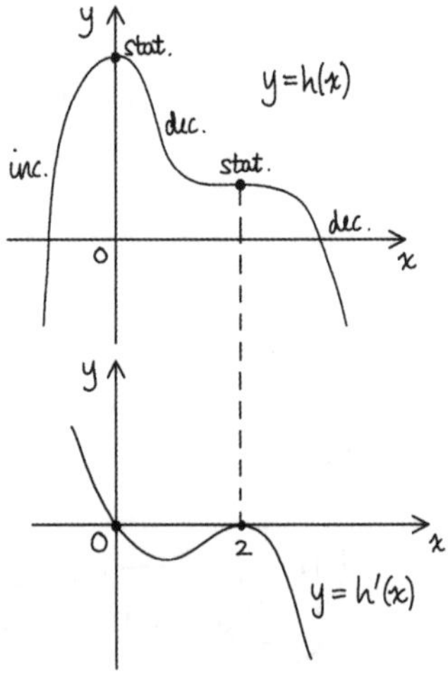

dec: $h(x)$ is decreasing so $h'(x) < 0$.
i.e. $h'(x)$ is below the x-axis.

inc: $h(x)$ is increasing so $h'(x) > 0$.
i.e. $h'(x)$ is above the x-axis.

stat: $h(x)$ is stationary so $h'(x) = 0$
i.e. $h'(x)$ lies on the x-axis.

b $y = 2 - h'(x) = -h'(x) + 2$.

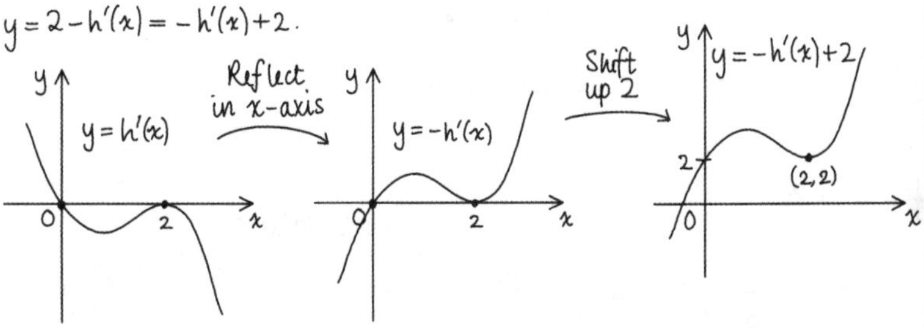

5

(a) See **Vectors** *§7 and §12*
(b) See **Functions and Graphs** *§8 and* **Polynomials and Quadratics** *§1*

a i

$$\overrightarrow{BA} = \underline{a} - \underline{b} = \begin{pmatrix} 3 \\ -3 \\ 0 \end{pmatrix} - \begin{pmatrix} 2 \\ -3 \\ 1 \end{pmatrix} = \begin{pmatrix} 1 \\ 0 \\ -1 \end{pmatrix}$$

$$\overrightarrow{BC} = \underline{c} - \underline{b} = \begin{pmatrix} 4 \\ k \\ 0 \end{pmatrix} - \begin{pmatrix} 2 \\ -3 \\ 1 \end{pmatrix} = \begin{pmatrix} 2 \\ k+3 \\ -1 \end{pmatrix}$$

ii $A\hat{B}C$ is the angle between $\overrightarrow{BC}$ and $\overrightarrow{BA}$.

$$|\overrightarrow{BC}| = \sqrt{1^2 + 0^2 + (-1)^2} = \sqrt{2}$$

$$|\overrightarrow{BA}| = \sqrt{2^2 + (k+3)^2 + (-1)^2} = \sqrt{k^2 + 6k + 14}$$

So $$\cos A\hat{B}C = \frac{\overrightarrow{BC}.\overrightarrow{BA}}{|\overrightarrow{BC}||\overrightarrow{BA}|}$$

Using $\underline{a}.\underline{b} = |\underline{a}||\underline{b}|\cos\theta$

$$= \frac{1 \times 2 + 0 \times (k+3) + (-1) \times (-1)}{\sqrt{2}\sqrt{k^2 + 6k + 14}}$$

$$= \frac{3}{\sqrt{2(k^2 + 6k + 14)}}.$$

b $$\cos 30^\circ = \frac{\sqrt{3}}{2}.$$

Exact values...

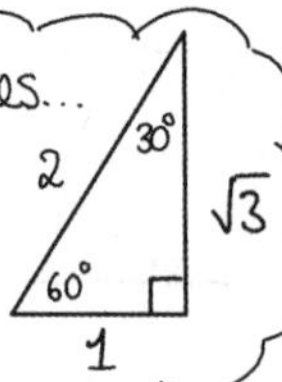

So $$\frac{3}{\sqrt{2(k^2 + 6k + 14)}} = \frac{\sqrt{3}}{2}$$

$$\sqrt{3}\sqrt{2(k^2 + 6k + 14)} = 6$$

$$6(k^2 + 6k + 14) = 36$$

$$k^2 + 6k + 14 = 6$$

$$k^2 + 6k + 8 = 0$$

$$(k+2)(k+4) = 0$$

$$k = -2 \quad \text{or} \quad k = -4$$

6

See **Sequences** §4 and **Trigonometry** §5

a For $0<x<\frac{\pi}{2}$, $0<\sin x<1$. So $\sin x$ satisfies $-1<\sin x<1$.

b **Method 1** $l=\frac{b}{1-a}$ with $a=\sin x$ and $b=\cos 2x$.

$$=\frac{\cos 2x}{1-\sin x}$$

Method 2 As $n\to\infty$, $u_{n+1}=u_n=l$.

So

$$l=\sin x\times l+\cos 2x$$
$$l(1-\sin x)=\cos 2x$$
$$l=\frac{\cos 2x}{1-\sin x}$$

Given that $l=\frac{1}{2}\sin x$,

$$\frac{\cos 2x}{1-\sin x}=\frac{1}{2}\sin x$$
$$2\cos 2x=\sin x(1-\sin x)$$
$$2(1-2\sin^2 x)=\sin x-\sin^2 x$$
$$2-4\sin^2 x=\sin x-\sin^2 x$$

Using $\cos 2A=1-2\sin^2 A$.

$$3\sin^2 x+\sin x-2=0$$
$$(3\sin x-2)(\sin x+1)=0.$$

$3\sin x=2$ or $\sin x=-1$ ← No solutions for $0<x<\frac{\pi}{2}$

$\sin x=\frac{2}{3}$

$x=\sin^{-1}\left(\frac{2}{3}\right)=0\cdot730$ (to 3 decimal places)

2012

7

See **Exponentials and Logarithms** – *(a) §5 and §3, (b) §4*

a The x-coordinate of T is the solution to $4^x = 3^{2-x}$.

Taking $\log_a$ on both sides gives

$$\begin{aligned}
\log_a 4^x &= \log_a 3^{2-x} \\
x\log_a 4 &= (2-x)\log_a 3 \\
x\log_a 4 &= 2\log_a 3 - x\log_a 3 \\
x(\log_a 4 + \log_a 3) &= \log_a 3^2 \\
x\log_a 12 &= \log_a 9 \\
x &= \frac{\log_a 9}{\log_a 12}
\end{aligned}$$

Remember
- $\log_a x^n = n\log_a x$
- $\log_a x + \log_a y = \log_a xy$

b $x = \dfrac{\log_a 9}{\log_a 12}$ for any base a, so let $a = e$.

Then $x = 0.884$ (to 3 decimal places).

So $y = 4^{0.884} = 3.41$ (to 2 decimal places).

2012